THE FINAL GIFT OF THE BELOVED

THE FINAL GIFT OF THE BELOVED

HER DISAPPEARANCE

13 DAYS

BARRON STEFFEN

The Yoga of Mindset Press
Kailua, Hawaii

Paperback ISBN: 978-1-951937-34-8
eBook ISBN: 978-1-951937-35-5

Library of Congress Control Number: 2020905698

References to the Siddha Yoga path and Gurus and quotations are used with permission of the SYDA Foundation.

Passages and references to the following works appear courtesy of their publisher/author:

I Have Become Alive by Baba Muktananda, published by SYDA Foundation Copyright © 1985

Sri Guru Gita, published by SYDA Foundation Copyright © 1972

"The Summer Day" from *HOUSE OF LIGHT* by Mary Oliver, published by Beacon Press, Boston Copyright © 1990 by Mary Oliver, used herewith by permission of the Charlotte Sheedy Literary Agency, Inc.

The Gift of Nothing by Patrick McDonnell, published by Little, Brown and Company, © 2005.

Book design by Colin Rolfe

Front cover image by Barron Steffen. Seana in Grand Teton National Park, 2009.

Distributed by Epigraph Books

The Yoga of Mindset Press
Kailua, Hawaii
theyogaofmindset.com

contents

preface

THIS IS A love story, although it is disguised as a tragedy. To the best of my ability I have shared the truth of what unfolded after my wife's fatal automobile accident. Following the thirteen-day arc from the moment I heard the officer say the words, "She is deceased," it is an honest and, at times, intense account. But it is unquestionably a love story.

This book is for you, dear reader. May it be of benefit, just as she was to so many in the world. Of course, it is also for and about her—my Seana, my Beloved, my Mooch, Amore mio, and my Muse.

Since *Siddha Yoga* is woven into every part of this book, it will be helpful for the reader to know a few things. Siddha Yoga is a spiritual path. It feels important to understand that it is a philosophy, not a religion, and it includes people from many different faiths. For myself, at its heart, Siddha Yoga sees the highest reality as divine Consciousness that dwells equally in all people. On the Siddha Yoga path, seekers come to recognize this, their innermost Self, experientially.

Please know that this story is not intended to promote any

spiritual path. Your approach will look different from mine. Yet without Siddha Yoga, I am quite sure that I would never have even met Seana, let alone survived the trials along the way. And I certainly would not have been able to meet this calamity and come to know it as something else entirely.

I have discovered the most strange and wonderful thing—that hidden within the death of a loved one may also be her final gift to us. And this is what I wish for you—in your moment of greatest need, though the world feels shattered into a thousand shards— may you remember this possibility and fully receive what the beloved longs to give you in farewell.

And so, in that radiant one's own words—*onward*. Together, you and I will take a journey that includes intense pain and emotion as well as great beauty and transcendent insight for, *nothing is as it appears.*

day one

1. The Final Break of the Intensive

THE MEDITATION INTENSIVE'S last break of the day was in the late afternoon. As I got up to stretch and walk around, I turned my phone back on and noticed a visual-voicemail message from a police officer.

That's odd, I thought, and went outside to my car to listen to it.

Sitting in the driver's seat, I put on my headphones and played it back. A Vashon Island police officer was asking me to call him back as soon as I got the message. I could not remember ever having been called by an officer before, and to have it come from the only policeman of the small island where my wife and I lived in Washington felt both noteworthy and worrisome.

Before I made the call, to steady myself, clear my mind, and return to a calm curiosity, I took in a few deep breaths. Then, still with some trepidation, I dialed the number.

"Am I speaking to Mr. Barron Steffen of Vashon Island?"

"Yes, sir. That's me."

"This is Officer Travers from the Vashon Island Police. Where are you right now, Mr. Steffen?"

"I am at the Unitarian Church in Seattle, sir."

"What are you doing there?"

"I am at a yoga and meditation retreat that's being held here," I replied, wondering why he would want to know that. For a brief moment, I considered sharing a more comprehensive version of the truth, but immediately abandoned the idea, having had so little success over the years in describing to others a Siddha Yoga *Shaktipat* Intensive.

"How did you get there?"

"In my car."

"What is the make and model of your car?

"A black Chevy Volt ... 2012."

"And what's the license plate number?"

I looked around inside the car as if I might somehow be able to see my license plate from the driver's seat. On the dashboard control display before me was the speedometer, odometer mileage, and other shiny black and silver graphics and buttons but, of course, no license plate number. I can't imagine why I thought the information he was requesting might be found there. But suddenly I felt uneasy about this call and a little scared, and I was not going to get out of the car to retrieve that for him, at least not until I knew more.

On the defensive and unaccustomed to being questioned about my whereabouts and license plate number, I asked him, "Why do you need that?"

Thankfully, he moved on to another question. "Are you married?"

"Yes, sir."

"What's your wife's name?"

"Dr. Seana Lowe Steffen."

"And where is she?"

"Seana is in Boulder, Colorado."

He had my full attention, now. Is this about Seana? As that thought arose, my body tensed in heightened alert amidst a widening fan of possibilities that I could not yet allow myself to consciously consider.

The officer continued his line of questioning. "What's she doing there?"

"Seana's been working on an environmental project for a few weeks."

"Does she live there?"

"No, she lives here with me." A perplexing feeling of suspense was slowing the conversation down like syrup, and a rising unease rooted me in the driver's seat. My chest, suddenly only half filling with air, compelled me to focus even more intensely in order to analyze his intent.

"Where is she staying in Colorado?"

"With friends in Loveland."

"Do you know where she is today?"

Something was definitely off, and I struggled to contain the anxiety now rising up like a giant snake slipping silently around my body, squeezing all the air upward and out of me. It was the randomness of his questions that disoriented and frightened me the most. *What is this about? Is Seana hurt?* Whatever it was, a sense of urgency verging on alarm was now tightly gripping me.

"Seana is finishing her work with the Natural Hazards Center in Boulder, Colorado, and flies back here tomorrow."

There was silence and a pause on the other end. Then, as if

he had decided something, he asked, "What time does your yoga retreat end tonight?"

"In an hour or two."

"When do you expect you'll be back in your home on Vashon Island?"

"I think probably by around eight tonight?"

"Okay. I am going to meet you later at your house on Vashon."

And now dread. The possibility that I might not be told until hours from now his purpose for calling and asking so many personal questions about Seana was unbearable. I categorically had to hear his words and could wait no longer, not minutes and certainly not hours. Nothing is real in this world, not even a death that happened hours before, until someone speaks it to you.

Inside of me a clear, unwavering resolve crystallized, and with it, all manners and etiquette instantly vanished. Right now, in this present moment, he was going to tell me why he had called.

"Officer, if this involves my wife, Seana, you need to tell me right now, not tonight."

"Yes, it does. Your wife was killed in a car accident in Colorado earlier today. She is deceased."

In spite of all the signals and warnings, I could not possibly have been more abruptly caught off guard. His words felt concurrently impossible and extraordinarily real. It was like falling off a precipice, but there was nothing left of the world.

Through my windshield I could vaguely make out the empty parking lot before me and white clouds in a blue sky overhead. Untethered, I floated within empty, endless space awhile, drifting among the folds of its silky fabric in dreamy cognizance of total disorientation.

Rippling out in deeper and deeper tremors and cascading across my consciousness were inaudible shockwaves. Paralyzed, my initial reaction was completely internal and mute. It was all happening very slowly, as if the terrible news was being passed by word of mouth deeper and deeper inside me, but it had so very far to travel.

Thankfully, there was no one around, not that I would have noticed. In my mind's eye, the trees and flowers outside the car appeared fuzzy and crossed up, tilting in the golden light of the afternoon sun, while inside me an irreversible chain reaction went through its invisible sequence. Trillions of connections within my brain were uncoupling, severing their relationships as fast as the uppermost edge of the sun drops below the horizon every evening at dusk.

No words approach what was happening inside me. There is so much power in words, and his were still landing far down inside me. Noiselessly, a vast inner horizon that, for as long as I could remember, had been the imperishable foundation of who I was, had simply vanished. And so had "I."

"Are you sure?" a voice asked him.

"Yes ... she is deceased," the officer replied.

Under the circumstances, these were the kindest words he could have spoken. *She is deceased* left no room for doubt. No hospital-bed vigil would change this, for no change was possible at all. Though seated, I was reeling.

I wonder if it's a norm in society that when, out of the blue, you are told your wife was killed today, no one has any expectation of how you speak or act after hearing it. And that's a good thing. It's not a point in time to suppress any part of the complex repercussions that have been set in motion. This moment will happen only once for both of you.

Downward, deep and wide, an uncompromising, utter finality began to vaporize all that had been so vibrantly present only seconds before. It was as if, mid-chapter, the next sentence in an engrossing book is, without warning, the very last one. It left so many unanswered questions and plot lines, all of which were now irrelevant.

In the stillness of the parking lot, sealed inside my car, there was no next thought and, as yet, no feeling. Or perhaps more accurately, I felt so very much all at once, but the feelings were so foreign to me that they had no names. For the moment, my sense of "I" drifted through my awareness as aimlessly as the sunlight that was filtering through the branches of the trees outside the parking lot in front of me.

And then, just as suddenly, "I" dropped down and back into my mind and body, obliterating everything on the path of return.

I CANNOT FOR the life of me remember what we said after that. No thought or feeling is fast enough to catch up to the expanding outer fringe of that detonation. I vaguely remember the officer asking about driving home safely. It ended quickly with something as absurd as, "Thank you for telling me."

As an elementary school teacher, I am quite familiar with the science of plate tectonics. At sea, when the earth's plates shift suddenly, tidal waves are generated, and a relatively common earthquake will push downward a section of seafloor that is hundreds of miles long and deep by an average of one yard, resulting in billions of cubic yards of water equaling trillions of pounds, all suddenly shifting positions. It is simple mathematics. If the relocation of those tectonic plates is in the upper magnitudes, the resulting waves will engulf and bury the land. At extreme volumes and amplitude, devastation is both inevitable and unstoppable.

Although no conscious thought had yet arisen in my mind, I

sensed a presence watching this through me, or as me, in detached fascination. There was a knowing. I knew an immense power had been unleashed inside of me, a tsunami of upheaval, and that it was only a matter of time before its arrival. The only question now was where should I be to receive it?

Unbeknownst to me, this intuition was a gigantic gift, a strong hand extended to me as I hung on the outer edge of the gaping crevasse, because it momentarily paused everything that was threatening to be swept away. Fanning out before me were all of the ill-fated options, senseless reactions like minefields in a darkened maze, each one awaiting its moment to be triggered. Though only vaguely cognizant of it at the time, it was that brief pause which allowed me to choose a different approach—to act, rather than react.

The possibilities spread outward from where I was sitting in concentric circles of alternate future realities. Instead of following my gut and plummeting downward into darkness and despair, it was as if I had been placed between two movements of a concerto and, resting in that grace-filled interval, I was pointed in a different and wondrous direction.

At the precise moment when so many strands of calamitous repercussions were present, this pause was to make all the difference now and in the course of my life after Seana, and following its path would end up offering me supreme protection, and much, much more, as well.

Inside the car in those first few seconds and minutes after the call with the officer, a velvety cocoon was forming around me, protecting me. I have no way of knowing how long I sat there. The car had become warm and stuffy, suspended in a timeless tableau, and inside and outside was all stillness. Within me, some inner accord between my mind and heart was permitting the unimaginable to soak in and saturate my whole being without a struggle.

When I heard the officer say, "She is deceased," something in me dislodged. Seana was the love of my life, my best friend, and infinitely more. It would take many books to impart even a glimpse of who she was for me and what we were for each other. I am reminded of that awestruck feeling of recognition when we first fell in love twelve years ago on my beach in Lanikai on the island of Oahu.

I say "my beach" because Seana had never been there before that day, and during the summer months I was there almost daily to paddle my surfboard out to the Mokulua Islands in order to stay in shape for the large winter swells of the North Shore.

On that particular afternoon, I was kneeling in the sand and watching the ocean, studying the timing of when I would take my paddle. To the left was the full length of Lanikai Beach, and directly in front of me was the vast afternoon palette of moving turquoise that seems to characterize this small stretch of the Pacific Ocean.

Nearly forty-five years old and still single, I admit that I was also on that beach that day for more than just a paddle. So, I immediately took notice when, walking up along the ocean's edge about thirty yards to my left, came a good-looking woman in her mid-to-late thirties. She did not look in my direction, and I remember thinking—*Attractive, right age, she has a camera around her neck. I know she can only go another fifty yards up to the right. When she comes back, I'll ask her if she wants her picture taken in front of the Mokuluas, and by her response I'll know if I want to ask her another question.*

Seana did indeed return a few minutes later, Nikon camera still around her neck. By then I was standing, and I caught her eye with that Hawaiian-style chin-up that can mean any combination of *Aloha, Hey!* or *How'z it?* When I asked her if she wanted her photo taken, I took note of the self-possessed sweetness about her as she passed me the large camera. Moments later, I must have said my smile-getting photo line, *You look marvelous,* because thankfully, she smiled.

Looking at it years later, the photo is quite an ordinary scene for Lanikai Beach. A beautiful, blond, blue-eyed woman is on vacation and standing at the water's edge with the two Mokulua Islands behind her. An amused, happy look on her face, Seana is nestled between the islands as if held within two folded hands and framed by the emerald green of the ocean and blue hemisphere of sky.

After the photo was taken I did indeed ask her many more questions, and the more she spoke, the more surprised and delighted I became. *Definitely intelligent, quite attractive, and charming, too.* In just a few minutes, I learned that she had already been on Oahu for two weeks in a yoga teacher-training and had another week of it before returning to her career as a professor at the University of Colorado at Boulder.

Though no plan had yet been hatched, crouching in the sand, I had to work fast—yet as slowly as possible. I knew that I wanted to stretch out this meeting, so I began to share with her all of the special places that she should visit before leaving.

"Have you paddled a kayak out to the Mokuluas, yet? It's amazing to look back on the island of Oahu from out there. And have you been up to the North Shore?"

I was well aware that I was finding her quite enchanting and soon noticed that I was dropping all my assets like stuffed wallets:

elementary school teacher, lived in Italy for years as a professional musician, fluent in French and Italian, daily meditator ... I also know that I was more than a little attracted to her because I took my shirt off, which, for a lifelong surfer was sort of like sending tanks into battle.

I ended up drawing Seana directions in the sand to all the extraordinary places she still needed to visit on the island before leaving, and we had our first laugh because it kept becoming more complicated as I added in the Hawaiian names of the high-ways and locations she would need to navigate. *Kamehameha, Kalanianaole, Laniakea.* Yes, they could be hard to remember. Perhaps she would like someone to show her a few of them?

IN RETROSPECT, IT'S as if Seana and I had come together later in life for the purpose of rekindling belief in the possibility of a rare and blessed life, a masterpiece of love and light. But hith-erto, neither of us had managed to breathe it into life. Seana was just exiting an unsuccessful marriage, and I was a lifelong bachelor. Neither one of us was willing to settle.

How does a human being learn to trust life perfectly, merging all of its glaring contradictions, and then bring that back into the world? In the other, we found a kindred spirit willing to focus on and explore the burning questions. Such that in due course it became instinctive for us to include within that growing edge of trust, not just the wonderful events of our lives, which was easy and deceptive, but also those other situations that arrived unsought. If it came out of the blue, then we agreed it was to be closely examined for hidden gifts and for the opportunity of unusual growth, no matter how incongruous or abhorrent it might appear upon first contact.

Though Seana and I were never on the same spiritual path, we supported each other in rising to meet the old, conditioned ways of responding that, at least in my case, would have been unimaginable on my own. Coming into harmony with battalions of hard-wired, negative patterns was like doing frequent tours of duty during a war—you had to be constantly willing and vigilant. And you had to have a wingman, a best buddy, a pure and loyal friend.

And so it was that, seated in the car after the officer spoke, something deep inside of me was silently waiting as patient as a seed. Perhaps long ago it foresaw this very moment of utter despair and had been lying in wait as motionless and undetected as water in a high sierra lake. For when the officer said those final words and the unthinkable became actual, like a key that is forged long before the gate or the lock even exists, something clicked perfectly into place.

2. The Unaskable Question

FOREVER. NEVER. To move from the impossible to unequivocally real in an instant was the piece that was taking the longest. It might take many years, but until more of it sunk in, I could not and did not move from my seat in the car.

Neurons were firing in places inside my brain that had never wired together before, and like honey dripping through a net, reconnecting to the other known pathways was a slow process. Moment by moment, my experience was subdividing itself into sequences of solitary stop-action frames. Each snapshot was an entire world unto itself, never again to be repeated or revisited.

I didn't think it at the time, but this could just as easily have been someone's description of an epiphany—the culminating experience of a lifetime of prayer, service, and meditation. Except it wasn't. It was trauma, and the inconceivable was unfolding itself, improvisationally rewiring my brain and identity.

Seana would have said that my reaction was the result of never having asked the unaskable question. In strategic questioning, yet another of her areas of teaching mastery, *the unaskable* is that question which, if unexamined, can threaten the foundation of the design of life in that realm. The fear of looking sets an avoidance pattern in place that jeopardizes the authenticity and integrity of the path.

I was sitting in the epicenter of the unaskable, and I was being effaced. If I were a planet, I am sure the view from outer space would have been of the entire spherical surface vaporized like a *Star Wars* movie.

When I eventually got out of the car, I instinctively turned in the direction of the church's main building. Dazed and sluggish, I had no plan and no thoughts. Soft currents of wind brushed my forehead and cheeks, and I noticed my legs somewhere beneath me. Looking from the inside out, or the outside in—I am not really sure—these first steps and physical movements felt like I had been drugged.

A patch of sunlight struck my head, reabsorbing me completely into a state of total quiescence. Moving forward into the wide-open space of the parking lot, something unearthed itself, presenting itself in me—as me. Unhurriedly, as if waking from a long dream, I found myself fiercely focused on one single purpose without a second. *Send Seana as many blessings as possible, as soon as possible.*

Alone at the edge of the walkway behind my car stood the local host for our Shaktipat Intensive. I had only met her earlier that day, but I knew that she had lived for many years in a Siddha Yoga *ashram.* So, when I saw her, I did not hesitate.

Walking forward to the curb until she was directly in front of me, I looked up into her eyes and said, "I need your help. I just found out that my wife was killed in a car accident this morning. I need to know if I should go right now and chant the *Guru Gita,* or back into the Intensive."

The look of sudden shock on her face confirmed all that was reverberating throughout my body and mind.

"Oh my god, I am so sorry!" she stammered. "How are you ... what do you need?"

As if my mouth was moving on its own, I heard myself say, "I'm also the *pujari* today. But I don't think I can do that seva, now."

"Don't worry. I'll find someone to cover for you. Really, you don't have to worry." Then pausing, she added, "I can't tell you what to do. But I do know that in this final video session, we'll be chanting the mantra with Gurumayi."

Hearing this, I knew exactly where I needed to be.

Leaving her standing there, I entered the main building of the church. A new stop-frame began like an empty question mark where each subsequent moment was equally unknown.

THE UNITARIAN UNIVERSALIST Church embraces diversity through an inclusivity of all faiths. It was a good choice for hosting our Shaktipat Intensive. Their site says, WHOEVER YOU ARE, WHOEVER YOU LOVE, AND WHEREVER YOU ARE ON LIFE'S JOURNEY, YOU ARE WELCOME HERE. We had rented their main building for this particular Saturday, and except for the seven of us taking the Intensive, no one else was around the church or surrounding grounds.

The main building had a central corridor with small rooms off of both sides. Leading from the main entrance back to the sanctuary and at the end of the central corridor was the great domed hall. It was a large, circular space with the pulpit directly opposite the entrance on the far side, raised a few steps above the main floor. For the Intensive, the windows had been covered with black plastic, allowing a better view of the video screen and also having the effect of naturally drawing you to a still place inside.

A room that is holding a Shaktipat Intensive is a

physical representation of the innermost sanctum of a human heart. Walking into the darkened hall, I looked toward the pulpit where the table with my teachers' photos along with flowers and candles had been set up as the front altar. To the left of it stood a large video screen. For this final break of the day it was projecting slow-motion footage of a rippling, open ocean surface in the moonlight with rolling, gentle swells in varying hues of silver, lapis, and purple. As if to echo my state, the night scene conveyed the natural chaos of the sea. Undulating and vibrantly alive, its dark blue expanse improvised in endless, creative beauty.

Normally, I would have stopped briefly upon entering the hall to touch the ground and then my heart, a tangible reminder that I was passing into a sacred space within the physical building as well as my heart. But I was in no condition to pause for this ritual. Glancing neither left nor right and disregarding anyone else who may have been in the hall, I moved straight ahead between the rows of chairs toward the front *puja*, or altar.

Entering the hall pierced any last lines of containment, and all of the mental and emotional boundaries that had been established over the course of my life were completely overrun. As I walked down the aisle, my head was pounding like a chamber in a cartridge that had been compressed far beyond its capacity. I felt like a grenade that might spontaneously explode at any minute.

My mind was frozen, cloven in two, while my intellect was in full-blown upheaval. I was vaguely aware that my body was not entirely under my control. Heat and energy seemed to be pouring into me from every possible direction, and buzzing vibrations were crisscrossing each other's paths, amplifying and overloading the connection between my body and limbs.

With my whole heart, I wish for everyone in a moment of extraordinary need just such a space of quiet, protected refuge. It can be recognized by a felt and spontaneous yielding of the heart, and in total candor it's not a place that first exists anywhere on the outside. It has to be created beforehand on the inside. Ironically, fortuitously, I had come to learn of my wife's sudden death while I was at a Shaktipat Intensive, the safest space imaginable and an atmosphere that had earned my complete trust many times over.

As soon as I walked into the hall, my breathing began to expand, and this in turn allowed some of the locks fastened so tightly around my heart to begin to loosen. Though I recognized the primitive, foundational need to surrender myself to the waves of grief pounding against the high cliff walls inside, even greater was the imperative to come before my teachers at this pivotal moment.

Instinctively, I knew there was a chance that they had a message for me, and in my extreme state it seemed more like something that they *had* to possess and pass on, because the blow was simply too great. So then, in a sacred space, might a deeper understanding not come in that very first glance? Some divine communication the instant our eyes meet at this tragic tipping point? Or perhaps a hint of how to persevere in such a time of uncommon need?

Never taking my eyes off the photos of my teachers, I slowly knelt down a few feet before the front edge of the puja. I could feel the wet tracks and burning sting of the tears streaming down my face, the rawness of unspeakable anguish, and my hands coming together in prayer position over my heart. The desolation that I felt was a physical, gaping wound that continued widening and expanding until it contained everything inside as well as outside of me. Raising my eyes to their faces, the immensity of this moment struck me like a missile.

Looking with great care, I searched their expressions like a starving animal for any scrap or intimation of a message. But for every desperate glance that swirled around and between us, it was as if they had resigned themselves to mute compassion.

Methodically, I took each one in turn starting in the middle with Gurumayi. Middle, left, middle, right; Gurumayi, Baba, Gurumayi, Nityananda. Then returning again in the other direction, back and forth, alighting momentarily like a bird on one after another and trembling so much that even on my knees it took conscious, sustained efforts to stay upright.

What message do you have for me? Surely you will give me some clue to the larger purpose—some understanding!

But their expressions did not change one iota. Darkness and light were in a stalemate, coexisting in almost intolerable tension.

Please, show me something to match the immensity of this moment—help me understand! I need you, now! This is beyond my understanding. I don't know what You want from me. What do You want from me? I give up. I give it up.

And still no inner word or vision came to my aid. I repeated these phrases over and over in my mind, unconditionally abandoning myself to them. Intense, nameless emotions commenced erupting inside like a ring of fire, little submarine volcanoes where each one followed the next in the string. They were like jagged fountains sequentially gushing out despair, hope, and hopelessness. Lightning in a night sky, mercurial arcs of heartbreak, sorrow, and love zigzagged repeatedly, wringing out every furrow and fold in my heart as if it were a wet dishcloth.

Yet, not even the slightest acknowledgment of my wretched condition could be perceived in my teachers' faces. The only clues I could discern were no clues at all, at least nothing that I was able to decipher at the time—expressions of an overarching contentment and empathy. I found this extraordinary, mystifying, and extremely painful, and it resigned me even more to the most basic truth. Seana was gone forever.

Across many years of *sadhana*, or spiritual practice, this lineage of teachers, these three Siddhas had become my central hub, such that even my wife had once asked me in exasperation, "Why didn't you ever become a monk?"

In my lifetime, I have had very few of what I would call supernatural experiences. Yet, years before I met Seana and while staying in the ashram, I had once been preparing for a morning *Guru Gita* chant by honoring the photos of the seven Siddhas, seven revered saints that are part of the lineage and tradition of my path. Their photos were hung successively along a side wall within the larger hall where the chant was held early each morning.

My regular routine at the time was to not move on to the next photo until I had felt a connection with the one I was looking at, some brief indication to help me infer that a confluence had occurred between us. I always tried to arrive early enough in the morning to have the time to do this without rushing.

Akkalkot Swami was an Indian saint from the 1800s, and in his portrait he is pictured standing amidst a dark forest wearing only a white loincloth with long prayer beads around his neck dangling to below his waist. The loincloth has dark stripes drawn along its edges. His incredibly long arms and fingers reach past his knees, and there is some kind of glowing, milky cone perched on top of his head. Like the sacred white ash markings spread across his face and body, I assumed the cone was drawn as a representation of his spiritual aura, which is sometimes done on the photos of sages in India. The cone has always looked more to me like a tall, white magician's hat, and his expression conveys an acute intensity and wealth of compassion.

That morning before the chant, when I came before his framed photo I focused on his face with great respect and love. Pausing for an acceptable sign or feeling that we had connected, I patiently waited. That signal could be anything—an emptying out of my mind, a tiny tap on my head, a honed clarity and focus.

In the midst of that brief lull and in the pause between my thoughts, within the picture frame Akkalkot Swami suddenly closed his eyes. Right in front of me—large, thick, beautiful black eyelashes swept slowly down and then, just as unexpectedly, rose up again restoring the photo.

Now, in the dim light of the Intensive hall, with all that had transpired today, I was hoping subliminally that something similar might happen. It certainly seemed possible. After all, wasn't this by far the greatest need I had ever experienced? Yet, no such miraculous gift materialized. Nothing. Given my extreme state of mind, it did not seem possible, and I found this, too, to be utterly astonishing.

AFTER A FEW minutes the bell rang, signaling that the break was ending. The final session of the Intensive was about to begin. I managed to stand up and return to my seat, hoping and resolving that no one would be sitting anywhere near me. Thankfully, with just seven of us in the hall, I had an entire row to either side of me, with several rows before and behind separating me from the nearest person.

The shaktipat mantra of the Siddha Yoga lineage is the Sanskrit *Om Namah Shivaya*. In the course of time, my understanding and relationship to it has evolved greatly. Early on in my practice, I was taught that to receive its greatest benefits, one should chant with the awareness that the mantra, the teacher, God, and one's innermost Self are all one and the same, and that its syllables are vibrations of God in the form of sound.

Over the years, I have chanted it many, many times for different purposes—enjoyment, growth, hope, protection, grace, to offer or receive blessings. In particular and most notably, I chanted the mantra whenever I was faced with personal crises, and this familiarity and intimacy had created a special bond that cannot be put into words.

Consequently, I chanted it when my four-year-old son was permitted to be taken from me by his mother to another state thousands of miles away by a judge who didn't know even the most basic guidelines or best practices of parenting. I turned to and counted on this practice when I was contemplating leaving my home to begin a new life, and then again upon arrival, landlocked and not knowing a soul beyond the one who drew me there. And I chanted it whenever (and far too often) fatalistic patterns of judgment, *samskaras*, took me to the brink of choosing to abandon the life-giving relationship that had brought me radical growth and joy.

By the time the final session of the Intensive began in the hall, I knew with absolute conviction that this was precisely what I needed most at this moment, the opportunity to funnel all of the shattered and splintering pieces that were hurtling chaotically through me into something that was strong enough to hold them, and that perhaps might even begin to heal them.

After quite some time, the syllables of the mantra gradually began to soothe and absorb me, creating a softness and tiny breach where minutes before there had been only impenetrable, caliginous fog. The strains of the melody ebbed and flowed, incrementally assuaging my scorched nerves and calming me down.

Nonetheless, I was having a lot of difficulty going deeper and staying focused. Momentarily in the eye of the storm, I was aware that I needed to let go and permit myself to be caressed by the sacred syllables. But while that was my clear intention, I was obviously still digesting the brutal knowledge that my wife was no longer here and would never return again, and the overwhelming pain and shock of that was just too fresh and raw for the deeper release I was seeking.

At some point, my focus began to shift away from my own experience of trauma and back to Seana. It's not that she had ever been absent from my awareness, but rather—being both the cause and the effect of the turmoil as well as central to the brunt of the assault that I knew was still to come at some point later tonight—I had set her aside. Now, all at once, she was vividly present in my feeling, and I began to weep for the first time. Great, convulsive sobs racked my entire body, and tiny explosions of light were detonating on the insides of my eyelids and brain.

How are you? Where are you? Amore mio, what are you experiencing?

Through the robust vehicle of the mantra, my attention was now turning fully onto her, and what arose caught me by surprise. I had presumed that returning inside the hall would begin the healing, but now, not only was the breach in my heart not mending, it was conversely growing wider and deeper until it became a bottomless abyss. For some time, I free-fell downwards through space, aware only of the mantra and the despair of great loss.

Then, quite unexpectedly, there was a sudden, powerful upsurge of intense love and gratitude for Seana and for who we had been and become for each other. Soon this feeling became so strong that I could not distinguish between the grief and the love anymore. It was as if the bottomless cavity that I had fallen into had not been a chasm at all, but a cavernous geyser, and now, gushing upward and through me erupted emotions of ecstatic love.

Once again, emerging into my thoughts came the urgency and longing to fulfill one sole purpose. *Send Seana blessings! Let this bring the highest blessings for her. Whatever You are asking of me, it is Yours. Just promise to protect her, bless her, guide her.*

Riding the syllables of the mantra like giant swells, they rolled through me as waves of intense love obliterating in my mind even the faintest possibility that there could exist any obstacle to her protection. They kept building and advancing until finally—a new, unmistakable understanding emerged.

Not yet, not yet ... enough now. You must not allow the fullness of grief and love to consume and swallow you yet.

The message was crystal clear, and I understood it immediately. Who knew how long this process, once set in motion, would need to be allowed to continue? The church hall was not a place where I could remain for long, and once initiated, the forces of emotion might be impossible to contain.

This morning I had arrived early to prepare for my *seva*, my service as pujari. The pujari has the role of preparing the *arati* tray with its offerings and the flame that symbolizes the light of the Self. The pujari then waves the flame before the teacher's photo at the beginning and close of the event.

During the chant, my news had gotten around to the others present, and near the end I was approached surreptitiously from the aisle. I suspect she must have been hoping to ask me if I wanted to wave the tray at the closing of the Intensive. But before she could get close enough to speak, I signaled her away with a deliberate, clear shake of my head as if to say, please don't ask me anything at all. These moments in the hall chanting the mantra were precious beyond measure. I couldn't possibly think or plan even seconds into the future. It was inconceivable that I could know what to do even one minute from now.

When, at last, the chant drew to a close, the suddenness caught me quite by surprise. Immediately recognizing the first notes of the ensuing prayer, its unmistakable melody was introducing the closing element of the Intensive. As soon as I heard it, I instinctively looked to my right toward the center aisle and saw the woman approaching the front of the hall to perform arati in my place. The silver tray was in her hands, and its candle was already lit. Instantly, the true significance and implication of the moment came into sharp focus.

This is my seva to complete, and today of all days, I must do it no matter how difficult it may seem right now.

Without another thought, I turned my body in her direction. Seeing me look up at her, thankfully, she paused, and I quickly made my way up the row toward her. She was standing very still and holding the silver tray out before her toward me. Without making any eye contact, I reached for it.

The instant I held the tray in my hands, I became aware of how shaky and unstable it felt to hold. Very carefully, I gently eased my fingers around the rim and between its grooves beneath the tray for a better grip. Turning toward the front of the hall to face the puja, I tried to gather myself inwardly. It felt like I was no longer in my physical body, and I absolutely knew why. I was the pujari on the day of my beloved's death.

THOUGH ONLY TEN or fifteen yards from me, the photos of my revered teachers appeared suspended and luminous, as if in another dimension. In fact, the entire area in front of me looked like a shining parallel galaxy, a bright hub at the center of a vast wheel bridging two distinct but interconnected realms. And in as vivid a change of scene as in any play or movie that I have ever watched, as soon as I looked upon it, a snowy, gauze-like veil fell away and my heart became filled with an indescribable poignancy and tenderness.

Walking forward to wave the flame, I was vaguely aware of myself. The experience of it was like wading deeper into a darkened sea and slowly being submerged. Now, it was all about maintaining balance: the tray with its candle held out sufficiently in front of my body and kept always perpendicular to the ground; my legs and torso supporting my shoulders that would steady my arms and hands; my inner mind that was in total disarray and observing all of this with resigned incoherence; and my heart that was unsure of anything and in awe of everything.

The photos of my teachers appeared before me. Their expressions had not shifted one iota. Full of compassion, they appeared to me like three swollen rivers converging in a storm, and before that holy confluence, I planted both my feet as firmly on the floor as I could possibly manage. All at once, while I was lifting the tray and flame upward to meet their eyes, in the midst of that gesture something abruptly snapped. It was my heart, and I felt it break quickly and completely.

Though it was not the last time this would happen, in that instant all hope departed in one swift acquiescence. In its absence, I saw that there was nothing left of me. There was no one left looking out of my eyes. Internally and externally, I recall only the glow of that alternate realm before me as visible—a *tableau vivant* composed of my teachers' faces, the warmth of the candlelight, and the stunning enigma and finality of Seana's sudden death.

In my hands, the arati tray circled slowly above their eyes and then around in an ellipse, again and again. Orbiting the images, the flame's luster refracted the candlelight with a golden glow, creating tiny ripples in the air. Throughout, I experienced myself as a tiny speck of dimensionless consciousness, adrift and floating through the vast ocean of the universe.

Outwardly and apart, I watched my body performing movements in an ancient ritual that was thousands of years old. Paradoxically, it felt both intimate and foreign, and I trusted it with my whole being. Gradually, the encircling flame carried me back to a semi-awareness of my body, and almost imperceptibly I began to pulse in and out from wherever I had gone. Having no desire to disrupt the sanctity and stillness that had come to pervade my senses in my absence, I instinctively began to slow the pace of the tray's revolutions in order to stay as present and unobtrusive as possible.

Awaiting me upon reentry, however, was a trembling body and a feverish head. Bereft of understanding and still waving the tray, I felt resigned and fearless like an animal that has given up all thoughts of survival and commits itself to the final task at hand. One last time, I returned to repeating in my head the words that kept arising inside me. Somehow they seemed to anchor me, as much as that was possible.

This is beyond my understanding. I don't know what You want from me. What do You want from me? I give up. I give it up.

The closing song ended. Utterly depleted and resigned to the unknown road ahead, I carried the tray to the rear of the hall and set it next to another photo of Baba. Here, near the exit doors, I turned to listen to Gurumayi's closing words in the Intensive video while gazing at Baba's face in the dim candlelight at the back table.

I remember she said that her love is always with us, and that whenever we love someone, we can recognize her love is with us.

She said other things, too, and I knew that in all likelihood they would be beneficial for me to hear right now, but I simply could not follow them. I was in ashes and embers, and ironically my state now perfectly matched my own earlier description of it. *This is beyond my understanding.*

Before heading through the exit doors, I leaned forward and felt for one last time the warmth of the flame, touched my heart, and turned and walked out of the hall.

3. India

THOUGH I DID not make the connection at the time, there was a very good reason that particular sequence of inner thoughts came up inside. Indeed, it was precisely why turning to those teachers had been so natural under the grave circumstances. Over the course of many years and long before Seana ever arrived, these three masters had proven themselves to me countless times.

I don't know what You want from me. What do You want from me?

This is beyond my understanding. I give up. I give it up.

These words first arose almost twenty-five years earlier when a judge gave full custody of my nine-month-old son to his mother, as well as permission for them to move three thousand miles away to Hawaii. I hadn't seen it coming and was absolutely devastated. Hadn't every child expert said the same thing in person and in print? A child should never be separated from a biological parent if they wish to participate.

Though my son was the result of a one-night stand, when I first learned about his impending arrival it galvanized me. I did not see it as random at all. Rather, it awakened altruistic feelings of love and profound purpose. The day after I was told, I remember penning an ecstatic letter to the universe expressing the exhilaration I felt at the prospect of sharing my life with him. Thus, when the shocking verdict came through, the judge's ruling shattered me, ripping away all sense of rationality because it seemed like such an irrational result.

Leading up to the court case, I had been so certain that the arc of the universe always bends toward justice. But now it appeared that sometimes it didn't, and since there was no knowing if or when that arc would touch back down, I simply could not comprehend a larger plan. How could it be in my son's best interests to move thousands of miles away from his father? What good could possibly come from that? With one stroke, all my inner landmarks of how life is supposed to be were erased.

After the call, I sat by the phone in silence. Instantly irrelevant, my beautiful plans dissolved like dirt and ashes caught in a rainstorm, never to be seen or heard from again. That's when the words spontaneously arose inside. Just before, I remember thinking, *This is insanity. There is no understanding this from a sane perspective.*

And then out loud and in short bursts, as if hearing the sound of my own voice could somehow help me comprehend the incomprehensible.

I don't understand. What do You want?

I don't know what You want from me.

What do You want from me?

Perhaps because the verdict seemed so thoroughly outside the realm of possibility, it did not feel odd to be speaking aloud to an empty room. I was just so unprepared. Bewildered and deeply disoriented, no other reaction was available to me in that moment other than a kind of dumbfounded astonishment.

During the weeks leading up to the verdict, my lawyer had

told me that, even with an uninformed judge and a worst-case scenario, they would never be allowed to leave the state. Given how estranged the mother and I already were, it would go against everything we had learned about best practice child-rearing. Having multiple parents who love you is a wonderful outcome for any child.

Accordingly, I had spent these last few weeks and months leading up to the court appearance readying life to share with my son, envisioning us living inspired lives and bringing out the best in each other. How could that be wrong? I hadn't attempted to take his mother out of the picture by asking for sole custody, nor would I ever, now or in the future.

The Venice Beach apartment where I was staying had glass sliding doors that open up onto the boardwalk and sand. It was a gorgeous California day, and the blue sky and shimmering ocean out front formed a flawless, temperate dome. Bright, yet cool and collected, nature was in total contrast to my state. I staggered outside and into the sunlight like a noonday drunkard, making it halfway to the ocean before collapsing into the warm sand and a small pool of tears.

That's when they began to echo inside. Like some novel mixtape confessing utter disbelief, an earnest prayer, and a white flag of surrender all in one, my own voice kept repeating in my head, *I don't know what You want from me. What do You want from me? This is beyond my understanding.*

Eventually one more theme arose—*I give up, I give it up.* Following the others in a repeating sequence, it was like adding a coda to a musical composition along with a D.C. *da capo*, so that instead of ending, they continued to cycle. Over and over, the loop replayed. Nothing could have stopped it, and since it was obviously stating the truth, I didn't even try.

Six months later, I got an invitation out of the blue from one of my best friends in Italy. Davide was heading to an ashram in India, and he wanted me to meet him there.

"Whose ashram is it?" I asked.

"Gurumayi Chidvilasananda. She's a fully awakened being. You have to come! She was passed the power of the Siddha lineage from her guru, Baba Muktananda, just as he received it from his, Bhagawan Nityananda. You need to meet me there. I'll pay for your ticket, so you have to come! Trust me, Barone. Just trust me."

As soon as I heard him say those names, I became intrigued. Twelve years earlier, I had met Baba in Santa Monica, California, and experienced a truly astonishing incident with him. So I knew that he was for real, and that therefore Gurumayi was likely to be as well.

I ended up staying in that ashram in India for forty days. The most truthful thing I can say is that something of life-changing significance happened to me there, and in the wake of the court's decision I was wide open to it. It was almost as if I were a freshly plowed field, and razed to the ground by the judge's verdict, whatever new seed was sown met no obstacle, since nothing else was present to compete for sunlight and water.

Looking through my journals from that period, there is a sudden and obvious sea change. All the pages from that point forward are filled with teachings and quotes from those three teachers and pithy anecdotes from ancient Indian texts like the *Bhagavad Gita* and *Jnaneshwari*. It seemed like every day I was struck by at least one new, stunning insight that felt pivotal to living a meaningful life.

From that trip forward, the practices of daily meditation, chanting, and study became my focus. I know that sounds strange, but in retrospect it was actually so simple. I fell in love. Deeply, head over heels in love. But neither with any individual, nor even the teacher. It was with *the teachings*. The more I tested them, the more obvious it became that until now I had been sleepwalking through life. I had always been so intellectual, so afraid to feel beyond a certain margin of safety, possessing many theories about life and purpose but with very few encounters of the heart. In the sacred atmosphere of the ashram, for the first time ever I was learning about love by actually experiencing it.

I remember one morning a few weeks into the journey. The Guru Gita was brand new to me, quite lengthy and in Sanskrit. Although I had read somewhere that Baba called it the one indispensable text of Siddha Yoga, I suspected that it would be the one practice that I would have little trouble dispensing with back home.

Yet one morning just after dawn, I found myself alone in the cool Indian air, standing beneath an outdoor speaker. An early recording of the Guru Gita was playing, and Baba was chanting it all by himself. I was completely mesmerized. After the morning's recitation in the main hall, everyone else had already dispersed into their day like seeds scattered from high altitude, but I was glued to the spot.

The Guru Gita literally means *the song of the guru*, and I knew Baba was singing to his own guru, Nityananda. In his voice I heard for the first time in my entire life the sound of someone deeply and hopelessly lost in love. It was unmistakable, and it utterly transfixed me. Devotion and longing oozed from every syllable and inflection. Never had I heard such tenderness, surrender, or trust. For a long time I couldn't move, and dared not, for it was like a revelation.

From that moment on, I was undone. The same can be said for the remainder of my time in India and many years after. In one sense, the shock and recognition have never left me. I realized that I wanted to sing like that, to live life like that—stripped completely of all pretense and to exist aware of only one thing—that I was unforgettably and irrevocably His.

Having been raised Catholic, and having left it as soon as possible, God was an idea and a relationship that I had cultivated purely on my own terms. Until then, my journals might contain a few devotional entries, as well as a significant increase with my son's arrival, however I had never considered the possibility that the One might exist *inside me*. But after the experience under the speaker, I gave myself to all three of those teachers and their teachings like a lover.

As the bright Indian days passed, the understanding slowly grew in me that there were no essential differences between us, and this was astonishing to learn. To pray or chant to Gurumayi was to be heard by Baba, my inner Self, Nityananda, and God. Nor was this an intellectual process. More than anything else, it was experiential, and it had to be.

In my past, I was always reading some book or another. Emerson, Goethe, Hesse, Yogananda, Jung, and many others passed before me—each one having its temporary effect yet never lasting. But that was definitely not the case here, and the main reason had nothing to do with my intellect. In fact, I wasn't really doing anything. Being in the ashram was more like sympathetic resonance, and I was a string on a musical instrument constantly being set in motion.

Daily, and more often than not, hourly, something would seize my attention like a mini-earthquake. Sometimes it was a tsunami sweeping me up and delivering me hours later in a wet heap. Tears became a regular part of my day. It was strange and wonderful, like falling asleep and waking up in a different world. I felt like an explorer, but instead of the sixteenth century, the Age of Discovery, and a big wooden boat—it was here and now, every hour. New trade routes were opening up bringing unimaginable wealth, and to be honest, up until now I'd never been too convinced such things actually existed.

If not for the fact that I was experiencing them, these were the stuff of a child's daydreams. They were the kinds of things one writes off as delusional, or laughs about with friends over a drink while finding minute discrepancies to prove the lie. And perhaps rightly so, for without actually experiencing them, fantasizing about their possibility is nothing but the purest of fantasies and of no use whatsoever.

Halfway through my stay, there was a four-day chant for the Indian holiday known as *Shivaratri*. It was ninety-six hours of nonstop immersion in the mantra, Om Namah Shivaya. Ironically, this was the exact same celebration and chant that took place when I first met Baba in Santa Monica more than a decade before. At the time, I did not grasp the significance of what happened between us, and with no one to explain to me the momentousness of his gift, I left his large, white tent more baffled by the experience than anything else. At the ripe old age of twenty, I chalked it up as a cool—if not puzzling—outlier and moved on.

But now I understood that I had received *shaktipat diksha*, spiritual initiation, and that it had literally catapulted me from one world into another. Although thirteen years would have to pass before coming to the ashram, I understood that my one and only interaction with Baba had marked the beginning of the true story of my life. And perhaps this was the most mysterious gift to come out of the entire crisis with my son, his tenacious mother, and the judge. It compelled me to reconnect with Baba through Gurumayi in India.

It also grounded me in the practices, and thank goodness, for I would sorely need them. For the next twelve years at a minimum, I was going to be put to the test over and again, calling on every ounce of grace and resolve. For the mother of my son was fierce, and she had it in her head that the only thing that needed to happen was for me to disappear. Consequently, along the way she was a formidable, mostly ruthless adversary, and used every means to that end, including dishonesty. Thus, when I moved to Oahu, even just to be able to see him took three separate visits to the Hawaii District Court.

Those trials were among the most extreme of tests, yet even more so were the daily ones. Such was her power that even with a court order, nearly every drop-off after school or aborted sleepover became a ferocious battle. Without the discipline of the daily practices to support and insulate me, I would have wilted in the face of her hatred and disgust. She was a bottomless pool of anger, relentlessly enraged at me for refusing to relinquish my knowledge of his existence and simply disappear into the storm.

With distance and perspective, I understand her actions and feel no judgment anymore. Love makes us do crazy things, and when combined with the tremendous fear of losing control, even crazier. Like a pilot entrusted with a precious payload, I think that she felt as if our son's life depended on her maintaining total control over him because, above all, she feared losing it and him to me.

On the final night of the four-day Shivaratri celebration, I chanted from midnight until the following morning with my dear Italian friend by my side, along with several hundred others. Then Gurumayi came out, and together we continued chanting for another hour or two. During the course of those final hours, I remember that Davide and I cried so much.

Directly across from where we were sitting was a large photo of Baba, and in the middle of the finale he came alive for me. With absolute clarity, his eyes conveyed that he was fully aware of what had transpired with my son. I had always been protected and guided, and always would be. And with that, the immense burden of the court case, along with its crushing sense of emptiness and defeat gave way like cracked, dried clay. The relief was tremendous.

In that moment, I suddenly recalled that in the two months leading up to the trial I had prayed to both Baba and Nityananda, and that this was one of the main reasons why I felt compelled to trust the outcome. As I looked at Baba that morning, he looked back at me with immense compassion, and mirth too. But more than anything, his gaze filled me with a love that I had never dreamed possible. He also seemed to know the answer to my question, *What now?* And though he did not share it with me at the time, it was clear that he knew.

Many years later, after Seana and I were married, she would occasionally express frustration with me regarding my daily practices. But other than love her with my whole being, and I did, there was nothing else to be done. These teachers and their teachings had long since become my central hub, and when you give your heart like that, there can be no question of taking it back.

A few years after meeting Baba in Santa Monica—yet before India, Gurumayi, or Seana—I was living in Italy as a musician. One day, I walked into a tiny English bookstore and a small, well-traveled book popped out at me. Like a thin, blue, hardbound reminder, this collection by the poet Robert Browning called to a part of me that had become mostly forgotten in the pitch and flow of European life as a pop singer.

In Browning's poem, "Rabbi Ben Ezra," I rediscovered something, or was tracked down by it, depending upon one's perspective. In a complement of words that, as much as language can,

describes flawlessly what smoldered deep and unseen within me,
one verse in particular captured it perfectly, reminding me once
again of my purpose for being here and the greater arc.

But I need, now as then,
Thee, God, who mouldest men;
And since, not even while the whirl was worst,
Did I,—to the wheel of life
With shapes and colours rife,
Bound dizzily,—mistake my end, to slake Thy thirst:

4. The Drive

O UTSIDE THE UNITARIAN Church and back inside the car, it was clear that I could not drive. I knew this was true because I just sat there. Immobilized and lethargic, I was aware that I had to get home and that this was the next step to take, but everything was in limbo. The willpower that it would require to drive the car was too great, and I simply wasn't ready to take that on yet. All I could do was sit there until something arose to replace my inertia.

After a while, the Intensive host came out of the building. She told me that I should not drive and I could come stay at her home for the night. This was the smart thing to do, and I honestly considered it. But like me, she lived on an island in the Puget Sound.

I briefly weighed the logistics and ramifications of attempting it. To pause my fragile state along with taking the ferry to and from her island and then back again to Seattle in the morning— all just to get back to where I was right now? It did not make any sense despite how precarious the alternative. And the thought of relinquishing the independence of my car, even temporarily, soon roused me to the only possible option. Right now, I had to summon whatever was necessary to somehow drive myself back to the privacy of our cottage on Vashon Island.

Outside, the sun was getting lower in the trees. I calculated the drive from where I was in North Seattle to the ferry dock would take forty to fifty minutes. Once on the ferry, a twenty-minute ride across the water to Vashon, followed by another twenty minutes to cross the island, and then I would be home. That felt absolutely right.

Looking around the interior of my car and down at the control panel, I surveyed my state and was pleasantly surprised to find that I felt as ready as I was likely to ever feel on this day. What I yearned for was a truly safe haven, free from any intrusion and distraction. Keenly aware that there was now something more important than the fear, I started the car.

Having seesawed for the last hour or so between the poles of despair and numbness, I found my sudden sense of clarity and action surprisingly comforting. It felt like the cottage was drawing me to it like the final destination of some unimaginably long odyssey.

Giant waves are coming.

As if from a great distance, they felt so close now that I could almost taste the salt and spray, the impending climax to an epic tale.

In the cottage, I will weather the building storm that is on its way.

In the cottage, I will send my beloved endless blessings. I will sit before my altar and ride out the swells marching toward me.

In the cottage, whatever needs to happen will happen.

As I SLOWLY backed the car out of its space and creeped toward the parking lot exit, I became hyperaware of two things.

First, my arms and hands felt very strange, as if they were not properly attached to each other. The joints between each section— shoulder to elbow, forearm to hand, hands to fingers, and fingers to wheel—did not feel connected. Gently flexing them, they did not respond as one single, integrated extension of my body and mind—so much so that, in those first few seconds as I slowly was navigating out of the lot, my control of the steering wheel felt alarming and dangerously suspect.

Just before exiting, I paused the car to inhale deeply before turning out and onto the first side street, hoping it would be sufficient to ground my trembling body and begin the drive.

There was a second concern, equally substantial. I understood that if I allowed myself to think or feel anything related to Seana's death during the drive—any of the loss, the love, or even the immense gratitude I felt welling up inside for her—it was likely that I would cause an accident. And since Seana was the only thing that I could possibly think about, it meant that no thoughts or feelings could be allowed for the entire drive.

Interestingly, as this understanding arose, it did not seem impossible, just absolutely necessary. And fortunately, it turns out that this unique task was something I had been training for—for a very long time.

THE YOGIC TEXT, *Patanjali's Yoga Sutras*, states that the purpose of meditation is stilling the thought-waves of the mind. Over the years, through daily meditation I had begun to experience myself as free for the first time since I was very young. Cultivating a daily practice, I learned what it meant to watch my thoughts. By slowing the mind down and witnessing my mental patterns, that pause both created and expanded gaps within the flow of my mental activity. In meditation, I would become filled by an innate, ever-present awareness, and over many years it left me with countless tangible experiences of what it's like to be free of thought, yet fully conscious and aware.

For the last twenty years, many of my summers had included a visit to one of my teacher's ashrams. While there this last summer, I happened across a quote of Baba's that would quite literally come to my rescue on this day.

In a question-and-answer session, Baba responds, "No matter what I say, the essence of all my teachings is that you should stay focused on the inner Self. You don't have to change your home or your society or even your manners. All that you need to change is your understanding of yourself. Always remain aware of yourself as the Self." What grabbed my attention that day was the phrase *the essence of all my teachings*.

Since first appearing in the West in the 1970s, this particular lineage of teachers has produced a prodigious treasure trove of what I consider to be essential principles for spiritual growth. I find many teachings almost musical in their ability to enchant and arrest my wandering mind and lead it to a better place. Still others, I find pithy and no-nonsense (actually I find them all to be no-nonsense, yet some teachings are breathtaking in their poetry), and each teaching has seemed to show up in precisely the moment it was needed, and not before.

At the ashram that July, however, I had no idea how critical this quote would turn out to be. At the time, I remember it struck me as the heart of where I wanted to focus and evolve, and over the two months that had passed since then, it had become something of a regular contemplation. Multiple times each day I thought about it, engaged with it, and invited it to enter more deeply into my subconscious.

Starting the drive home, I understood the precipice I was now on. Yet there was really no other option available. If merely thinking and feeling could be hazardous to others and myself on the road, I decided that this quote would be the one thought I was going to allow myself as I drove. If any other thoughts or feelings of consequence arose, I would replace them with Baba's words.

Please know that I strongly do not recommend driving in any similarly traumatic situation. Yet, as I'm sure you can imagine, in moments of deep despair one must naturally defer to whatever knowing he or she has access to at the time. I knew unequivocally that the most pivotal action I could undertake was to get myself to the protection and isolation of the cottage to meet the mounting waves that would soon reach their apexes.

As someone accustomed to riding surf of a Hawaiian scale, I possess vivid, occasionally nightmarish memories of the sheer power and raw fear that nature and water together command. So that driving out of the parking lot, it was as if I had been dropped into the ocean far out to sea with nothing visible in any direction but one—the cottage.

INSIDE THE WARM, stuffy cockpit of the car, I took complete refuge in Baba's words, repeating them over and over to myself. As soon as any thought or emotion related to Seana's death threatened to catch fire, I returned myself to those words. So much seemed at stake, and the sheer intensity of inner and outer concentration that was being generated after only a minute or two was astounding, and this was going to have to be sustained for the next hour.

Shortly, I was turning onto the freeway. Merging with the on-ramp, a strong surge of anxiety rose up from inside.

There would be so many cars all moving and shifting their positions at speed.

This is so dangerous!

Focus. No thoughts.

Keep your awareness on your presence, your inner Self, the simple fact of your aware existence.

Then, out of the blue and amidst all my apprehension, something wonderful happened. I found a freeway filled with evening traffic, so that by the end of the on-ramp I actually had to slow down to merge with the other cars. Seeing automobiles crawling along the interstate, stretched out before and beside me, a softening and almost blissful relief spread throughout my entire body. It felt extraordinary. My neck, shoulders, arms, and hands actually relaxed and loosened up, and for the first time since leaving the parking lot, my breathing deepened. And with that, a thawing ever so slightly began to filter its way through the dense tangle of fear and tension that had quite literally frozen my limbs.

With freeway speeds hovering around twenty miles per hour, sometimes slowing to almost zero, I would not have to drive the higher speeds any time soon. Nevertheless, the fragility of my inner condition and the larger reality that I was suppressing made me extremely aware that I still needed to remain hypervigilant to the constantly shifting traffic. Although for several years now, my capacity to abide in a watchful state free of thoughts for a minute or so at a time had been growing—that was always in peaceful environments, not driving on a freeway where lives depended on it.

As I drove, I kept repeating Baba's words many times. *The essence of all my teachings ... stay focused on the inner Self.* I noticed that, as I was repeating the words mentally, it felt as if a luminous sheath of protection was filling the inside of the car all around me.

As long as I did not think or feel anything related to Seana, this translucent membrane pulsed larger and smaller like something soft and alive. Though surrounded by cars all moving at different speeds, at times it felt like I was gliding through emptiness. I witnessed in awe as eddies of silence emerged from inside me like dark galaxies in the canopy of deep space, each one encircling and shepherding to safety some extremely fragile aspect of my mind and heart.

Given the grave context, the moment-to-moment attention required to drive while simultaneously holding at bay every thought and emotion was all-consuming. Yet from another perspective, it was spellbinding. To be using what I had practiced every day for so many years, and for that very training to be crucial to my survival was extraordinarily thrilling.

It also made me wonder. Was it working because I was so desperate and without any other alternative, or was it effective because necessity and nonattachment are doorways that make the unimaginable possible? Rolling down the crowded freeway where the only permissible action was to vigilantly watch my mind, I also caught glimpses of a mysterious, unidentified piece of myself that seemed to be observing this whole interstate experience with an aloof fascination.

As I came closer to the ferry dock on the west side of town, I realized that it would be wise to stock up on food here and now, rather than on Vashon Island. It seemed very important to arrive home fully prepared for whatever the next phase would bring with as few distractions as possible. The main supermarket on Vashon Island was a place where I was likely to run into familiar faces from our school community. I absolutely wanted to avoid that.

The West Seattle supermarket was nearly empty when I

entered. The very first thing I noticed was how surreal it was to be shopping. It seemed almost unconscionable to stop now and feign in public that I was in any condition to shop. Entering the store, I felt like an actor who was expertly hiding his identity as well as a harrowing secret, and I remember walking up and down the aisles, pretending to be in a normal state of mind for the benefit of any passersby.

To say that this interlude was eerie and strange would be a gross understatement. I roamed around the market concealed and disguised, and split into two personalities. The first was stunned and in shock like a wild animal, and the second was flabbergasted at my expert, improvised performance. Soon I had the shopping cart packed with enough frozen food for two weeks and fresh flowers for the puja, and I quickly made my way to the checkout stand.

Glancing at the checkout woman, I wondered if she would be able to tell that I was hiding something or would somehow be able to intuit my false front, thinking to herself, *There is something just not right about this guy.* What would I do? In such close proximity, it felt impossible to conceal. Yet mercifully, she took no notice of me, and I was quickly back on the road and at the dock within just a few minutes.

PULLING INTO THE line for the ferry, it was now dusk. At some point in my drive and shopping spree the sun had set, and I had not noticed. Although there was still a twenty-minute drive on Vashon Island, I knew that this chapter was done. The perilous drive was complete. Somehow we had made it here.

Since I first heard the officer's words, there had undeniably been a sense of *we* sprinkled into the moments. I don't mean that I felt Seana's presence, nor that some higher being was riding alongside me (although that may have been true—who can say?)—but perhaps the twin acts of holding the gravity of my emotions at a safe distance while another piece of me was positioning to be able to receive them created this feeling of duality.

Halfway up the ferry dock and stationary for the first time in hours, the ferocious grip I had maintained around my mind and heart began at last to subside. Amid the fading light, as I sat in the car waiting for the ferry to load—great, invisible cracks within me began to expand. Almost immediately, an immense, ineffable sadness flickered to life like candlelight within a darkly shuttered room.

Looking up at the sky, the evening was already glittering with the light of many stars. Far out amid its vastness and wild beauty, all at once I was sure that I could see my first glimpse of Seana's elegy brilliantly flashing forth, and it stung so bittersweetly that for a few seconds I could not breathe.

THE FERRIES THAT connect the islands of Puget Sound and Seattle are large, multileveled ships comprised of three tiers with the bottom two tiers holding 90–120 cars at capacity. Each ship has a large seating area on the top floor for food, bathrooms, and sightseeing. On the dock that evening there were only a few cars waiting for the next ferry, and I didn't have to wait long before we were shuttled into the lowest tier along the ship's railing.

As the car came to a stop, I looked out the window and over the guardrail at the night sea. Only a few cars were ahead of me and none behind, and it began to appear as if each occupant was choosing to head up to the main galley. I felt truly grateful for this.

It was entirely dark now, and the only visible light came from the crescent moon and its reflections upon the hull of the ferry,

the immense sea, and great meadows of whitecaps. A stillness set-
tled upon me, and in that brief pause a palpable shift in my conscious awareness tore through like a sudden gust of wind. Quite
unexpectedly, I found myself reaching for the handle to go outside.
I was completely unprepared for this, and at the first gap in the
door, the wind buffeted me backwards. I needed my whole body—
all my arms, hands, and legs to successfully exit the car. Coming
from the insulation and warmth of the car, each of my five senses
awoke into action.

The sounds of ocean and wind were everywhere, as were their
physical sensations. It was literally like passing from one dimension into another. Foamy, snow-white spray was bouncing off the
hull of the ferry and producing a rhythmic, white hissing sound.
Around and beneath the vessel, the tumult of seawater struck me
with a brace of cold, open-ocean air. Nature's elements suffused
every particle, and it stirred me deeply.

The transition from inside to outside was also a virtual one, so
that I found myself standing at the threshold of a gate that had
been patiently awaiting me for hours. Inexplicably, I had somehow
understood that this gate was not to be approached until I was in
solitude and fully prepared to meet what was on the other side.

All around me the sea and sky were alive in unceasing motion.
It was like standing in the eye of a hurricane where stillness was
a passageway into the center of the maelstrom. The ocean was lit
with a glowing luminosity, and its expanse before me clashed and
gyrated with coarse, crushing sounds. The outer scene's chaos and
upheaval perfectly mirrored the chaos and tumult within me.

Without any warning and as if its appointed time had been
reached, whatever inside me that had been holding back this
moment came loose like a small clump of dirt in a downpour, and
with that passage now liberated, into the opening rushed a grief,

primal and profound. Along with it came a fierce resolve to surrender completely, to embrace one last time both my wife and the terrible truth, and to join with her in never again being the same. In seconds, the narrow breach had already grown a hundred times in size, and the release that poured through was abrupt and feral.

Not only did I accept that pact, but I welcomed it. To let go and disappear forever, to give my full consent and vanish, soaring out over the black sea into the night sky—this felt true and right, for my heart could not possibly hold the immensity any more than a teacup could contain the boundless ocean. How *do* we venture out beyond the invisible boundaries of our understanding? In truth, I have no idea, and can only guess that love does it.

One by one, the swells within me now rose up like advancing mountains to their fullest cresting peaks and came crashing down. As they did, it drew out a sorrow as old and vast as the sea and sky before me.

I think grief may be one emotion that all creatures share. It must be because it wasn't just that I sobbed in excruciating pain, it was also *the sound of it.* I was wailing like an animal. Coming from within me in the form of protracted howls and cries was the loss and longing of irrevocable separation and the inexpressible agony of heartbreak.

These sounds were totally unexpected—so unusual that I vividly remember standing there at the railing and being pulled outside of body-awareness in wonder. From this vantage point, I saw myself to be simply another living thing grieving the loss of its life-mate. I wondered how many creatures since the beginning of time had felt this same emotion, crying out and howling in long, sustained hues. This threnody of lamentation poured itself through me, spilling out into the windswept ocean and sky.

Words fail to have meaning in this place. Sound alone was the purest and most human expression of my grief, and I abandoned every part of myself to it. Gripping the railing with both hands, I called out the names of my beloved.

Seana! Amore!

And began calling out to my teachers, *Gurudev! Muktananda! ... Gurumayi! Nityananda! I need you now!*

I am with you more than ever, and I am more broken than I ever dreamed possible.

I beg you ... be present now.

I am begging you.

Be present now with both of us.

I DON'T KNOW for how long I called out to them like this. I can honestly say that it was an event unlike anything I would have ever imagined possible. In a first reckoning and a true one, it brought together powerful, opposing forces and used them in unthinkable combinations. Chaos and longing, defeat and purity, they were like fireworks destroying themselves together. Conjoined, they created something even more extraordinary, so that here she was—raw, unparalleled loss and her eternal companion, imperishable love.

On a nearly empty ferry boat beneath a deep black dome littered in shimmering stars and halfway across the Puget Sound, formlessness burst into form and cried out. Then, like a giant, invisible snake undulating its way across the vast open ocean, she withdrew again. I emerged from it with the excruciating understanding that my Amore was now en route, traveling her inverse path from form back into formlessness.

So THEN, I wonder, which is it? What is more real—appearing or disappearing, birth or death? Who can possibly say for sure which one is the truer reality and which is the dream?

The ocean passage and its uncompromising release had gifted me a provisional peace and a natural pause in the action. Enough to catch a deep breath before the next wave, which would come who knew when? But at least now I had been forewarned. *Be ready for anything.*

Before long, I saw the approaching ferry dock of Vashon Island. Fleetingly, it struck me how strange it was to be traveling all alone to our island. Only a few years had passed since we came across this channel for the first time, hand in hand, and it had been only a few weeks since we sat together delighting in this very trip across the Salish Sea. But I am in neither world now. And I suppose the same is true for Seana.

5. Vashon Island

L IKE A PLINIAN eruption, the ferry ride had liberated an enormous amount of suppressed emotion, and so the brief drive to the cottage was already proving to be a much less stressful one than its predecessor on the I-5 freeway, both physically and mentally. Muscles and limbs that had once throbbed with tension were now feeling but a tiny fraction of the anxiety and dissent that only an hour before had posed a real threat. Even my forehead, which had been as overheated as a July thermostat, was significantly cooler, and an aura of grave inevitability now pervaded my night drive, pulling the car forward like a giant magnet.

The two-lane highway that splits the island is predominantly lined by tall pine trees, and after an initial illumination on the north ferry dock, it is almost entirely unlit until you arrive at the small town of Vashon about halfway to the cottage. Along the way, towering evergreens stand at attention like enormous soldiers over long swaths of country road. On a brightly lit night, the highway is fringed in moonlit dark blues and greens with tree lines casting long, outrageously misshapen shadows. Beneath tonight's polished sliver of a crescent moon, I felt their presence like a community of elders, as large trees seem to epitomize. So that slipping underneath the branches of the great guardians, it seemed as though they were reaching out to embrace me and offer their heartfelt condolences as I passed.

Once beyond the cluster of lights and four-way stop that mark the modest nucleus of Vashon, I prepared myself to at last listen to the phone message from the Boulder County Coroner's office. Already waiting in voicemail for several hours, it had been lurking in the back of my consciousness like a dreaded, unopened letter all through the lengthy drive.

Though brief, listening to it added yet another layer of dream-like impact. Merely hearing the coroner leave her name and number struck me with remarkable force and jolted me awake to the grim facts of the drive. As I moved closer to home amid the familiar night vistas, each view was a stark and fleeting reminder of the radical shift in reality that now permeated our island paradise.

Taking in deep breaths and gathering any last remnants of courage and strength, I called the coroner's office back. In the sort of voice that does this for a living and understands how difficult it is for the caller, she told me succinctly, gently, and factually what she knew of the fatal accident.

In Boulder, Colorado, around 10:00 a.m. this morning on a county highway that we had often driven, another car crossed into Seana's lane and hit the Prius head-on. There was no explanation of why, except that it appeared as if no drugs or alcohol had been involved. She added that Seana had apparently tried to swerve before impact, but was unsuccessful. She was rushed to the emergency with a sporadic pulse that doctors briefly maintained but then lost. Driver number one was not injured, and Seana was dead.

Coming over the hill that leads down to Quartermaster Harbor and the cottage, I knew that this news had to be shared with others, but I had no idea how that was going to happen.

Obviously, it had to be soon. Most immediately pressing was to communicate with our friends in Loveland, Colorado, for they would be expecting Seana to return home later tonight. I knew that I could not let them worry as the night progressed and Seana did not show up.

Sharon was one of Seana's closest colleagues and friends, an incredibly grounded and reliable woman, and her family was dear to us. Since moving a few years earlier out of our 3,000-square-foot home in Longmont into the 480-square-foot cottage on Vashon, they were our go-to in Colorado. And because the entire footprint of the cottage was smaller than our master bedroom had been, they generously allowed most of our home to be stored at their farm.

I was well aware that the news I had to share would initiate in them a cascading sequence of intense grief, but I was incapable of thinking beyond this to any other options, nor could it be put off. It felt vital to handle here and now—and clear the way for whatever was going to happen at the cottage.

Sharon's familiar, friendly voice answered. It sounded like she was in the car with her children and husband, but I couldn't let that stop me. They had to be told.

"Sharon? I need to tell you something, and I need to just say it. Seana was killed in a car crash today."

In the split-second gap between my speaking and her first words, it was as if I could see her pain coming across the great distance of a frozen tundra, gaining in momentum until at last it merged with my own in the present moment.

"What? Oh my god, no—No!—No!"

I could hear someone in the background, doubtless her husband, asking what was wrong, and then Sharon, incredulous, "Seana was killed in a car accident today!"

In my first real conversation since the police officer, absolutely unfit and unable to process the pain that was on the other end of the line, I repeated to her as concisely as possible what the coroner had shared, and then said, "I am so sorry, but I can't talk anymore."

It was all I could get out. Almost to the bottom of the last hill before the final turn toward the cottage, an irresistible, overwhelming current was pulling me onward like some tremendous gravitational force. I knew that I needed to retreat from the conversation as quickly as possible and prepare myself for arrival at our home.

"Can you please tell Cyndi and Kelly—and ask them to help tell others?" I asked.

To put it mildly, this was a lot to ask, and by tomorrow morning it would become quite a division of labor among dear friends, but I was approaching my final destination. It was yet another incomprehensible ending strung beside what was to become a long string of them. Blunt as a mallet, I had nothing left in reserve for our dear friend, Sharon. Empathy, the impact on her family, the shocking news would all now billow out to others like frothy, filthy backwash into the sea. At least for this evening, we each would need to sail a while longer alone.

A stone dropped into a serene lake causes ripples on the surface of the water to emanate outward from the point of disturbance. Unlike that, the ripples of Seana's death would extend far beneath the surface for many people across the globe, upsetting many lives. But tonight, there was nothing more to be done, and I couldn't possibly, anyway. I was in shock and survival mode, and less than a mile from my destination.

THE PUGET SOUND is an inlet of the Pacific Ocean and made up of a miraculous, complex system of interconnected waterways.

This area is at the heart of the Cascadia subduction zone, where one edge of two massive tectonic plates, the Juan De Fuca, is being subducted beneath the North American Plate. Also known as the Salish Sea, the Puget Sound's basins and underwater sills are carved in a unique, intricate lacing of land and water, the result of constantly advancing and retreating ice sheets over several glacial periods.

Our cottage is located on the eastern shore of Burton, a small community about halfway between the north and south ends of Vashon Island. Its broccoli-shaped peninsula juts out into a narrow strip of the Puget Sound sitting at the isthmus between Inner and Outer Quartermaster Harbor and connecting on one side with Maury Island. About a half-mile wide at its widest point, the inlet extends 3.5 miles between Vashon and Maury islands with massive Western Red Cedar, old-growth Hemlock, and Douglas Fir trees lining the shores.

A few years earlier, Vashon's one public elementary school had offered to fly me in from Colorado to interview for a teaching position. This final interview was to consist of teaching a lesson to a fifth-grade classroom on the next to the last day of the school year. Seana and I both realized that I might very well be offered a position that same day, so we had prearranged with a local realtor to take us house-hunting as soon as the interview ended.

The cottage was the third or fourth house we saw that afternoon. It cannot be seen from the road nor from the top of the wooded hill just above it. As we walked down the dirt and grass path between tall pine trees and saw it for the first time, the tiny home was perched on pilings and hovering magically above the Sound. It looked like a green, undersized water spider relaxing on the sea.

Our realtor looked back at us and said, "This is a really tiny cottage, not even five hundred square feet, and it has some serious problems and risks. I don't think it's what you are looking for, but it was on your list, it's on the water, and has a certain charm."

Built in the 1930s as a fishing shack, twice each day the tides circulated in and out beneath it. The cottage, and especially its pilings, were in serious states of disrepair. Of the thirty or so still managing to hold it upright, eighteen pilings needed to be restored and half of those replaced entirely. Like a cartoon where beavers gnaw logs to fine points like sharp pencils, several had gaps of daylight between their tops and bottoms. Yet, as soon as Seana and I saw it, we knew. It had such potential. Within a day, we had entered into negotiations on it and accepted the teaching position. By the end of our second year, Seana's remarkable vision had transformed the cottage into an elegant, mostly solar-powered, tiny oasis.

ALTHOUGH THERE WAS no such thing today, pulling into our wooded driveway hours after the fact would be a victory in itself. But the amazing feat was not well-celebrated, or at all, probably because the closer I drew to home, the heavier the burden had grown. It was a trade-off. Like an engaging action movie that temporarily suspends one's awareness of a nagging physical pain, the sheer danger and intensity of effort to be driving under these circumstances had provided total, compelling distraction.

Turning off the car expunged with a harsh finality the paper-thin veil between my awareness and the unambiguous reason that I was here. Like a heavy curtain that had been blocking out the morning sun, any last interference fell away, and I was acutely, lucidly aware that there was nothing left to do. And with this, an indescribable, bitter sadness now arose from what it actually meant that I was sitting alone in our car in the driveway in the dark.

Through the front windshield shadowy outlines of tall pine trees wrapped everything in a syrupy, rich silence. Somewhere below them down on the water was the cottage. All around, both inside and outside the car, hummed a strange, dark stillness. Illuminated in bits and pieces by stars and moonlight, our grassy knoll shone forth with a soft luminescence so that I had the distinct impression that I was perfectly alone, yet not unaccompanied.

Though the transition from driving to now merely sitting still had been as smooth as the dark mirror of water that waited below, there was also a surprising abruptness to it. Similarly, pairs of opposites were emerging everywhere. For example, despite the fact that despair had so saturated my body that I could literally feel it coursing through my fingers, arms, and face—I could not help but marvel at the obvious presence of gentleness. With surprising tenderness, it escorted the jagged undercurrent of bitterness into the new, uncharted territory like a well-mannered and compassionate chaperone. So, though I was bereft to the core, I did not struggle.

Poignant did not just gain a fresh definition from these contradictory emotions, but rather opened wide its arms to this new visitor and revealed an entire, unique, alien world of stunning beauty. Of course, this moment had always been coming. Yet, I was wholly unprepared for the paradoxes or the opulence of its bittersweet taste, which was so unlike anything that came before or ever would again.

Walking down the grass pathway from our wooded parking area, I kept gazing up at the star-filled night sky over the tops of the pine trees and between them down at the water of the Puget Sound where our house is found. Deeply disoriented, it felt as if I was wandering in some parallel universe that was both immensely beautiful and terribly sad. Somehow, I had become hopelessly lost, and now I was trying to comprehend where I was and how I had gotten here.

To someone unfamiliar with its pier-like design, the first view from above might appear as if the cottage was floating on the current, unmoored. And maybe on another, more subtle level it actually was, but what I recall most about that first glance was its timelessness. Intersecting below me was the past, present, and a suddenly vacant future—and together they were all coalescing into one indelible, unforgettable image.

Now halfway down the stairs, seeing our home come into view below me was so unexpectedly jarring that I had to stop and stare. Somehow, the cottage was a perfect reflection of my state. Small and pale white, the house looked isolated and empty, like a hollow ship adrift on the sea. Its lovely charm had been converted into something sad and fading, as if from another time. Three of its four sides were surrounded by water, and tonight a shimmering path of light was darting from the sea directly toward it so that it looked like a brilliant fuse lit by the moon.

Paradoxically, this all felt strangely familiar and foreign at the same time. How familiar and precious this cottage, the latest and unexpectedly final iteration of our love story. In my mind, it had grown as inseparable from her, and us, as the soaring, poetic correspondence that we exchanged when we first fell in love—to wit, Seana had once shared one of my early messages with her mother, whereupon my mother-in-law-to-be responded back, "So, what's it like talking to yourself?"

Therefore, how suddenly foreign and unfamiliar appeared the dark silhouette below me on the water. Wasn't it only this morning that its beating heart, Seana, was marked in attendance somewhere on the planet? I stood there on the stairs above it like an infant blinking people and things into and out of existence. For there was the cottage, still solidly present, but now it appeared as an untimely monument that had been sculpted and delivered too soon.

I HAVE A very clouded recollection of the ensuing sequence that night. I do not remember entering inside, and only vaguely recall preparing the altar and then chanting the mantra until fatigue overcame me not too long afterwards. Days later, I took a photograph of the puja table so that I am still able to piece together some of that brief night.

Centered and encircled in the picture like the hub of a radiant wheel of light is the framed wedding photo of us on our beach in Lanikai where we met and were married. In the image, we're wrapped together by an extra-long tropical lei, and we each have one hand gently touching its fragrant white flowers and the remaining hand out of sight, holding the other's. Expanding outward from its center like rays from the sun are pictures of my teachers and the Siddha saints, a lit candle, an incense stick, and the bouquet of flowers from the market.

I do remember at some point going to bed with the overwhelming feeling of a dizzy, glazed exhaustion that coated and penetrated me like sunstroke. Taking with me our cat, Kaulana, along with a stark, grim sense of irony, I knew that when I awoke, for a few seconds I might not initially remember that today my beloved had disappeared. But that the sweet ignorance of sleep would only last a few fleeting moments.

DAY TWO

6. The Cottage

WHEN I AWOKE Sunday morning, no tender moment of innocence awaited me. It was still true. I was as certain of Seana's death as the night before.

The cottage, however, greeted me with a gentle mixture of profound stillness, the sounds of nature, and bright morning light. Along with me, the cat and natural world were stirring, welcoming the dawn with their own musical score of near-silent yawns from tiny jaws, ocean tidal movements, and the cries of countless sea birds. Lying there, it all fused seamlessly into a surprisingly serene sense of spaciousness.

Down here on the water there are only three houses, with ours in the middle. In all directions, the stamp of the natural world pervades. Across the inlet on Maury Island no other beach homes are visible, while a few are randomly scattered above the bay like fox burrows hidden within the slope of a mountain. As is often the case for many weeks in fall and winter, no one was home in either of the other two cottages, so I was alone and indebted to the privacy and protection of nature.

I let the cat out and filled her bowl. Kaulana was the perfect companion for this rite of passage. A magnificent gray and white Siamese-lynx with Lanikai-blue eyes, she had come into our lives by accident a few years before and had been adored ever since. For the next five days, her detached, calm presence was to be a healthy balance to the extremes of my experience.

As I prepared to sit for morning meditation, my mind went briefly to what it imagined its other duties were today and then began to scan for what would need to be done. Word would be spreading of Seana's death, and I understood that I had to tell Seana's mother as soon as possible before she found out some other way.

WHEN I WAS in the ashram in July, one of the things I made sure to do was meet with a woman whose role for several years had been to help those whose loved ones had recently died. She assisted devotees in understanding what supports they might choose from and which spiritual practices they could offer at the time of death to bring blessings and grace to the one who had passed. At the time, I had asked to meet with her because my mother seemed to be approaching that threshold-time in her life.

During our lunch, Mary reminded me that in Siddha Yoga the most auspicious and beneficial action to take upon learning of the death of a loved one is to chant the Guru Gita on his or her behalf. Its sacred syllables and their vibrations carry an immense amount of grace and can help the departed individual

navigate the transition from form to formless life. This centu-
ries-old Sanskrit text was first introduced as part of the ashram daily schedule by Baba in the 1970s.

Mary also shared with me the concept of thirteen days.
In the mostly Hindu tradition, a person is mourned for this
period, and on the thirteenth day a ceremony and celebration
of life is performed to honor and invoke blessings for final
release from anything that may be holding that person to this
physical world.

Sitting for meditation this morning, I found it to be
uneventful and quite disappointing given the gravity of events.
Although I have been taught the importance of remaining detached from judging my daily practice, the fact was
that, much like my experience yesterday of returning into
the Intensive hall for the chant, I still held unrealized hopes
and expectations. In meditation, I found it difficult to go any
deeper than surface level, and for the entire hour my mind was
neither malleable nor still.

Afterwards, I took a pause to eat something, assess my
day, and send off an email seeking support from one of the
monks in upstate New York at Shree Muktananda Ashram.
Aside from the one call that unquestionably had to be made
to Seana's mother, Swamiji was the only other person I could
envision wanting to speak with today.

Soon afterwards, I sat for another round of the Guru Gita.
As it progressed, I was easily distracted by thoughts and noticed
a core physical exhaustion. And even though tears spilled forth,
cascading down my shirt and onto my lap, by the end it felt
inadequate and decidedly incomplete. I wondered if harboring
the clandestine desire that something be revealed to me was

instead impeding the very thing I yearned for. Somewhere within the randomness, I felt sure a larger plan was concealed.

In the tranquility following the chant, I quickly became lost in thought. I began to wonder what Seana might be experiencing. Is she feeling lighthearted and free? What is this transition like for her, and where is she in the process? Is she thinking of me at all, or is she already detached from the physical world and moving onward?

The truth was, I had no idea. I could only stick to the plan of offering as many blessings as possible and rededicate myself to remaining as present as possible in my heart, rejecting nothing and noticing everything. And while I did not relish the idea, it was indisputable that Seana's mother needed to be told as soon as possible today.

As I contemplated what would be the best approach, I grew increasingly troubled. How do I tell the mother of my wife that her only daughter is gone? And what might that unleash in her? This truly concerned me. If my own anguish was any measure, then there had to be support for her in place. Gradually, a plan emerged.

JANA STILL LIVES on the farm in central Ohio where she raised her two children, Seana and Seana's younger brother. Though now alone in that house, part of her family still lives within a short walking distance on a companion parcel within the large, rural property. I concluded that I would need to tell Aunt Shelley and Uncle Gary first and ask them to be ready to support Jana afterward when I called her with the news.

In a crisis, timing matters. You take a leap and count on others for help, even though they, too, are likely to be thrown into grief and shock by the news. The first responders—they are the ones who must be sturdy enough to bear the initial brunt so that others in more fragile positions, swept up in the fierce current of their emotions, have the best chance to ride it out in a safe and supportive environment.

Aunt Shelley and Uncle Gary were the ones for this job. Two down-to-earth, sensible human beings who had been part of raising Seana, they knew her and loved her unconditionally.

I gathered up my courage and nervously dialed the number.

"Hi, Uncle Gary? It's Barron calling."

"Hey there, Barron, good to hear from you! How have you been?"

My voice and hands were trembling. In that moment, fully aware that I was about to change his life, what else is there to say but the truth? It was like diving into an abyss or intentionally taking a knife to someone.

"Uncle Gary, I don't know any way other than to just tell you this. Seana was killed yesterday in a car accident."

"Oh ... no. Oh, no. No! Seana, no. Oh, Barron, no!" The tonal peaks and valleys in his few words were a glimpse into the sound of genuine heartbreak. I could hardly bear it. From the small space of serenity that I had just spent so many hours carefully cultivating, I was instantly towed back under by the fresh turbulence, corkscrewing downward into darkness again along with Uncle Gary.

In the background, I could hear Aunt Shelley, alarmed by her husband's tone, asking, "What? What's wrong? What's wrong? Is Barron alright?"

And then Uncle Gary was in pieces. "Seana was killed in a car accident yesterday!"

The woeful cadence in his voice conveyed such a raw

intimacy that it was as if I was listening in on the sound of a heart breaking. I could feel his insides peeling away from his body.

In the background I could hear Aunt Shelley using almost the same words as Uncle Gary in a heart-wrenching mirror of the same stammering, broken patterns of collapse and all-encompassing grief. To witness it, and in part to be the cause of it, was to relive the agony of the moment when I was first told. It was an excruciating price to pay. At an unearthly speed, utter despair poured through the modulations and inflections in their voices, telling a tale of total desolation.

When there was at last a pause, I began to share what was known of the accident. I told them about the plan and how I needed their help in telling Jana. She couldn't be alone after my call. The idea was for me to phone her in thirty minutes, little time for them to manage their own trauma, I knew. But we were all aware that any delay was not in Jana's best interest. So, in half an hour they would walk up to Jana's house, wait silently by the front door and listen carefully for a sign that she had been told. Then enter and take it from there. This would also give me some time to prepare myself.

Dear, dear Jana. The first time Seana's mother came to Colorado to meet me, she got me alone in a car and basically threatened me.

"My daughter is head-over-heels in love with you. I have never ever seen her like this before. I need to know your intentions. Do you love her? If you don't, I want you to tell her so as soon as possible. Then, you must leave immediately. She will grieve, and she will be heartbroken, but she will move on. Her divorce last year took a lot out of her, and I will not allow you to hurt her more deeply."

A mother tiger protecting her thirty-eight-year-old cub. Jana usually went straight to the point. I found it both winning and awkward all at the same time.

At the half-hour mark, breathing deeply, I gathered myself and dialed her number.

"Jana?" That was all I could manage to get out.

"Barron! My favorite son-in-law. How are you?"

This was a favorite quip of hers with me. The fact is that I am her *only* son-in-law.

Summoning a blend of grit and recklessness that I hoped would permit me to speak at least one clearly articulated sentence without a complete breakdown, I said, "Jana, I need to tell you something, but I need you to be sitting down, first."

"Okay, dear one, let me get over to this soft, cushy chair, right here, and ... there. What is it, my angel?"

My chest beat its frenzied protest, and I leapt off the precipice.

"Jana ... Seana was killed in a car accident yesterday. I'm so sorry."

"What? ... Oh, no ... No, no, no!"

And then, from wherever I had gone to be able to deliver such news, I was violently thrust back into the present moment, and like a dam that had been compromised too many times, I ruptured again and easily. Now, my own sobbing combined with hers, and we were swept away in a torrential confluence of immeasurable love and loss.

Soon, through the phone, I heard a loud knocking at her door, and the voices of Aunt Shelley and Uncle Gary.

"Jana? Jana, we're coming in!"

And then I could hear the sound of the front door opening with the voices of Aunt Shelley and Uncle Gary jumbled together and frantic, "Did you talk to Barron? Did he tell you? ... Oh, Jana, oh Jana!"

In came the cavalry, as broken down and grief-stricken as the one they had come for. They were one family, sharing the brutal burden in the most human of ways—in each other's arms, and I knew it was done.

SINCE YESTERDAY, MY phone had already recorded many voicemail messages, but I could not bring myself to listen to them. Nor would I for weeks, and in some cases, months. Over the course of these initial days, it would become both peculiar and educational to observe myself reacting to ordinary, everyday things quite differently than my established routines.

Seana would say that, above all, I am a creature of habit, and it would be said with mirth, laughter, and a rolling of her heavenly blue eyes. She would add that atypical responses are to be expected under such exceptional circumstances. Yet, what may have seemed obvious and to be expected by others had now become an unpredictable, new ingredient of my daily existence. And just like the metallic blue Morpho butterfly that enchanted my days as a seven-year old, the oddest things would captivate my curiosity and metamorphose into observable truths. Nothing was normal anymore. Or, as I remember my teacher once saying, "Nothing is as it appears."

So, although I could not possibly listen to even the shortest of voicemail messages, I found that texts were for some unknown reason permissible. Perhaps it is because they are short, have no soundtrack, and hence no real depth. Much to my surprise, I found they uplifted me, and the ones that I did read seemed to help me process in unexpected ways the extreme, uncharted nature of my ordeal.

Though it may sound odd, it never occurred to me that I would need anyone else to get through this. Seana was the only person in my life who had ever fulfilled that on-demand role. So, what a wonderful development to learn how much I could benefit from others' words of concern. The occasional text seemed to filter through just the right amount of muted emotion, heartfelt interest, and detachment, and did not overwhelm me.

I found that I could read a text at any time, as well as choose not to respond. Emoji also proved to be an uncomplicated tool, for they conveyed the essence without getting bogged down in speech. Knowing that a particular person had made an effort to convey his or her sincere condolences or support, yet having the power to limit the effects, was a perfect fit for the rhythms of grief and solitude.

LATER THAT MORNING I opened my computer to check if Swamiji had responded. I was both relieved and unsettled to find his response. He was someone I had known since the mid-1990s, and as is often the case when sharing a spiritual path over many years, he had grown into both a mentor and dear friend. But seeing his sweet, compassionate communication, now I knew I would need to call him back. And even though I had been the one to reach out, the prospect of speaking about this, even to him, flustered me. I wasn't sure if I was ready.

Dear Swamiji,
I write in the hope that you will join me in sending

blessings to my wife, Seana Lowe Steffen, who was
killed in a car accident yesterday while I was taking
the Intensive. No expectations. I honor you as a
dear friend.
Barron

*

Dear Barron,
It took me a while to take in this news. I send
profound condolences to you. What a shock. I will
definitely send prayers here at the Temple. If there
are other ways I can support you, please let me know.
*   I will be in and out this evening and tomorrow—*
but if it would be helpful to speak, please feel free to
give me a call—even in the middle of the night.
Best regards and much love,
Swamiji

I was thoroughly unprepared for the impact of his response. Having no idea just how much an acknowledgment of my situation could mean, my powerful reaction caught me completely by surprise, triggering a series of emotions that quickly exposed the brittle illusion that I had been subtly weaving. Filled with self-reproach, I saw that I had in fact been hiding from the fullness.

In a later conversation, I remember Swamiji describing what was going on. "You don't want to pole vault your feelings with the practices." In a sense, this was exactly what I had been doing. What else did I have to hold on to? From the first moment I heard the officer's words—one-pointed focus, meditation, chanting, and prayer had been guiding and protecting me, and they had kept me away from the abyss. It was understandable, of course. I was in well over my head and heart, and I knew it. But there needed to be a balance.

Now, as if in answer, an immense gratitude and transcendent love swept me up like an all-powerful gust of wind that until this moment had remained in abeyance. Precipitous and abrupt, I was like a toddler surprised and humbled to find herself tumbling down a flight of stairs. A great flood of tears began pouring out from some unidentified wellspring inside, and it forcibly directed my attention inward to the gaping hole of sorrow.

It was as if I had never felt great loss before and had neither wept nor understood the deeper purpose of weeping or its true power and beauty. But wasn't it only last evening that I clung to the railing of the ferry, staggered by emotions that were so new they had no names, and so powerful that I had disappeared and gone who knows where? Hadn't I wept, then?

Then I saw that these tears had little to do with Seana. Instead, they gushed out as an expression of indebtedness for the Swami's compassion and concern for my loss. As I would come to discover over the course of this process—after Seana, almost any gesture of human kindness or gentle words from another could tap that enigmatic inner reservoir. Unexpectedly, it would release a surge of tears and even wrenching sobs. There were times that I would have to remove myself as quickly as possible from a setting in order to be able to manage it. Yet, in truth, I also slipped away so that I could more fully savor its nectar. Each time, it was like being filled by her great goodness and radiant love.

After many similar occurrences, I finally put it together that great loss must be the best friend, ever-present companion, and eternal beloved of love, because like some omniscient presence, it always knew. Even before I would become aware that a heart-string had been touched, my breath would catch in my chest on its way out, stuck halfway between my navel and my head. Then the gates of my heart would fling open.

Over the next year, this was an experience that repeated itself many times. I would find myself in the most unlikely places where the simplest acts of human kindness or humility, unexpected and unlooked for, would freshly crack open my heart. All at once, genuine wonder at what I perceived as the unassailable purity in others would move me deeply. And right there in a checkout line, the man with my groceries would speak gently, free of expectation or calculation, and it would unlock storehouses of the purest ambrosia.

These tears were also noticeably different from the others. Like a characteristic fingerprint, they had a purity and intensity that was distinct. Entirely free of wanting or self-interest, they felt almost like a high. In fact, the experience affected my body awareness as potently as any drug ever had. Suddenly, I would feel intoxicated with love and gratitude, and for as long as the experience held me close, grief was nowhere to be found. It felt drunken and blissful, and very similar to being wrung like a wet towel where the tighter it is twisted, the more intense the release.

It was unmistakably love, and in the guise of others it would arrive soft and taintless as evening light to touch my heart like a tangible reminder of the nobility and divine ancestry that flows through all of humanity. And ultimately for me, it was simply Seana, in them and as them. She was the cracking agent, the solvent.

To perceive my Amore's divine virtues suddenly flashing within, and as a total stranger, was magical. I found myself wondering, *How and why is this happening to me?* Eventually, I came to understand that Seana and her divine qualities had completely infiltrated me, soaking through countless layers of selfishness and ego. Through the mysterious process of her disappearance, and like a catalyst in resin, I was pushed to experience her virtues as if they were my own. And though I felt like I had no right to them, for I had not earned them, love said otherwise.

7. Swamiji

A BIT LATER in the afternoon, when I had finally calmed down and eaten something, I felt like I was ready to call the ashram. I decided that I would record the call and tell Swamiji at a later date, because the odds of my remembering the important parts of this crucial conversation seemed about as likely as my cat making me my morning espresso. The exchange was simply too important.

"Swamiji, it's Barron calling. Thank you so much for responding."

"How are you doing?"

"You know, it's a back and forth, for sure. Yesterday, protected by the mantra and my own awareness and all those things ... It's ironic, I spoke to Mary before I left the ashram in July. I was asking her how to give blessings when someone dies because my mom is at a certain age."

In my mind, I felt clear about what I wanted to say, but my words were coming out scattered. It was a struggle to stay with just one line of thought, but I knew what I wanted to ask him.

"So, I've chanted the Guru Gita already many times and I'm chanting the mantra, and I just want to know—how can I give the maximum number of blessings to this being who has departed?"

Gently, Swamiji responded, "Well, there's nothing like the Guru Gita."

"Over and over?" I asked.

"Normally after thirteen days, we kind of feel the soul is ready to move on. There's a celebration of life on the thirteenth day. You might want to just do the Guru Gita every day for her. And if you want to do it more than that, you know, you can. But just doing that every day with the full intention will be a great blessing. And, you know," Swamiji paused for a moment before he went on, "you're going to have to figure out a way to fill your days. I'm sure you're just full of all sorts of emotions."

"I'm going to take a leave of absence. Fifth grade started about two weeks ago, and I am going to take a leave. I don't know how long it's going to take. Her body is in Colorado. She was there when she had the accident, so I'll fly out in the next couple of days to cremate her, and all those things."

"When did you hear about it?" Swamiji asked. "Did they call you out of the Intensive or after you'd gone home?"

"No, it was during the last break. I had a message from a local sheriff here on Vashon, and I went out to the car on the break and called him. He asked me questions, 'Where are you? Are you driving?' And finally, I said, 'You just need to tell me!' And he told me. And when I came out of the car ..." Momentarily lost in that scene, I struggled to pick up the thread once again.

"I was in such a state, and I told the local host. I asked, 'Should I go home and chant the Guru Gita right now, or come into the Intensive?' She said we were about to chant the mantra with Gurumayi, so I went back in and chanted the mantra.

Then, I made it home and got on the ferry somehow. I don't know how."

"I really feel for you. I can't imagine what it's like. Your whole insides must come out."

"I felt like vomiting numerous times."

"God bless you. I shared it with the Swamis, and they put their hands over their hearts. They're going to send their blessings too."

"Thank you, thank you," I replied, feeling indebted and profoundly grateful.

"So, I would say do the Guru Gita every day, and if you want to do more, that's fine. Just feel what your inner being says. You can always do *japa*, too, repeating the mantra silently and dedicate it for her, as well as chant the mantra.

"I didn't know if Seana was in the same town with you, and I was thinking, *Oh my god, had you just left her for the day?*"

"No, no—she was in Colorado. It was the last day of her trip there. Things had gone so well, and it really felt like a new era. We had just celebrated our tenth wedding anniversary and her fiftieth birthday two weeks ago."

Gradually, I became aware that there was something I needed to better understand through the vehicle of this conversation. I had numerous questions, but which were the most important ones to ask?

"I guess what's happening with me is that ninety-nine percent of me is completely taking refuge in the practices, and thank god I've been so disciplined for so long. But I guess there's a part of me that always hoped and wondered if the Guru Gita wouldn't also protect the ones that I love from calamities? Obviously this is her *karma* as well, but that has shown up a little bit too, I admit."

"The thing is," he said, "you have to believe everybody does have their own destiny. The scriptures do say everyone has their own time." Then adding, "We don't know what blessings are. We can't see the full limit of blessings."

"Yes … yes." I was following closely now.

"You know, if you're looking for silver linings, she had twelve great years with you."

That struck a chord. "Uh-huh," was the best I could manage.

"She left in a good state. You know what I mean?"

"Yes … yes." This felt important and true, but I couldn't fully understand why.

"So in a way, she was in an expansive state."

"Very much so." He was going somewhere with this, and I was trying to rally my mind to stay with it. I could sense that there was something specific in this thread that I needed to hear.

"And so, thank goodness for that, you know? If I were you, I would do the Guru Gita, and I would also sit down before my puja and invoke her—talk to her. Let your heart talk. Express your love to her. It can go on for a few days, and at a certain point say, 'I want you to enter the light. That light, that love of God, is where I will meet you. That's where I am too.'"

"Beautiful!"

This was making so much sense to me. I could feel the frayed connection between Seana and me growing stronger and deepening as he spoke. It was as if the bright opening of a field in a dense forest had suddenly appeared after a long period of darkness, and I was being resuscitated back to life.

"I would have that dialogue because I suspect her spirit is looking back at you now. I suspect she's with you. So, I would have sessions where I would talk to her, and let her know all

75

you're feeling. Then at a certain point, express your gratitude and admit that your love is eternal. It's beyond the body, you know? Give her your blessings to move on, and that you will see her on the other side." He was expansive now, compassion oozing from his words.

"She's there, and she's worried about you. She's probably been traumatized, you know? That's why the mantras will soothe her soul, and then open her to the light."

I felt truly excited. I also sensed our conversation was coming to a close, and I wanted to try and gain as much clarity as possible before we hung up. All of this resonated deeply, and I knew it was what I needed to hear.

My days and nights in the cottage must now include communicating my love and gratitude to Seana on a regular basis. I would be with her and be available to her more fully. I also sensed the formless presence of some, as yet unknown, remarkable possibility in all this.

"So, must I be chanting the mantra with great intention, or can I be listening to it?"

"I think what you want to do is dedicate it, make an intention. You could say, 'Now I'm going to chant the mantra in order to send blessings to my wife.' You can bring your mind back to that and just try to become absorbed in the mantra, but in a relaxed way. Not like—I've got to or it doesn't count!

"Because you know, it'll also be good for you. I'm sure ... I don't think traumatized is the word, but you know, you're heartbroken in some ways."

That stopped me. I was stung by the plain, brutal truth of it. I also became even more aware that I had been hiding, shielding myself from what it meant to be utterly broken and shattered. Yet, I *was* heartbroken, and no prayer, meditation, or chant could shut that out completely. Indeed, that kind of avoidance was the antithesis of what these practices provided me. Quite the opposite of concealment, they removed obstacles to self-trust. They unveiled.

"Only that light can heal," Swamiji continued softly.

Moved to my core and almost unable to speak, "Yes," was all that escaped my lips.

"And it's going to take time. It doesn't get over in thirteen days or one year, or whatever. It's just time. The light is the one thing that can heal. We're all on this earth for a limited amount of time in this body."

"Right."

"And when you realize this is the play of God, when you have that perspective, then you can be happy and free. So by sending those blessings and praying to God for your wife, she can open to that light. Then, she'll understand the larger play."

"It's ironic because my biggest prayer for her this summer was, 'May Seana experience the heart and love of Siddha Yoga.'"

"Well, so maybe she will? We're going to be offering prayers for her from the Temple."

"Thank you!"

"We're going to send beams of light to her. You know that may be the greater karmic connection between you."

"Right," I answered, accepting this as a possibility.

"There's a book called *Life between Lives*, and it talks about a psychiatrist. He interviewed people who'd had a death experience and seen the greater arc of their soul's journey. All we can do, regardless of the intimacy of our relationships, is to contribute to each other's light on that bigger journey. You certainly offered that to her."

I had indeed been thinking about the karmic commitments

that Seana and I shared. Had we perhaps agreed to contribute to one another's growth before we were born into this particular incarnation? Now it seemed more possible than ever.

My small, individual perspective was literally being stretched beyond capacity by this conversation. But instead of agonizingly painful, on the contrary, it was inspiring and uplifting. Perhaps it was because I was starting to let go of my concepts of what I should and should not be experiencing. This conversation was helping me realize that I needed to shift my thoughts and actions away from just grief and love and express them in a different way. Though appropriate at the time, this felt truer than my previous approach—more expansive and loving, and it was a direction that I wanted to move in straightaway.

Compassionately, Swamiji continued, "This is a time where she's looking at the energy that comes from you. So, it's important to do it relaxed, with love." Stifling a chuckle, he added, "Not like a Zen monk, you know?"

When Swamiji was a young man he had spent time studying in Japan, so I could imagine why he found Zen monks humorous, having almost been one himself.

"You have the energy of the *shakti*, and you can invoke the grace and make that intention. Those mantras will soothe her spirit, and then she'll feel that reconnection with you. She'll know that it's okay to open to that other light that is coming to her."

"Yes, beautiful. I'm so grateful." I really was. His words felt auspicious and timely, and I knew our conversation was coming to a close.

"Well, feel free to call me anytime. I mean it."

Barely escaping my lips, I managed, "I'm so grateful for your friendship."

"Likewise, and I really feel for you, brother."

Now, scarcely audible and almost overcome, I whispered, "Thank you."

Swamiji let out a sigh of empathy, "I'm trying to see the greater arc. The mystery …"

"Mmm." When he said, "see the greater arc," it was as if the roof of a house had been ripped away and light spread into every corner of it at once. I suddenly recognized what had been niggling at me the whole conversation. His natural grasp of a much larger picture was pointing me directly toward the greater arc of a human soul existing beyond just this one physical life. Seana was much greater than this one incarnation, and far more than my wife. She surely had lived many, many lives.

I would not have thought it possible for me to be pushed over another precipice and to freefall through even more layers of dark void, but when I heard the Swami speak of the greater arc of the soul, it was as if my small frame of perspective shattered into a thousand pieces. And in its place, the sketch of a much larger outline came into view.

Until this moment, I had been so bound by small, extremely limited ideas of myself, of Seana, and of this world. I had imagined that my grief and love were expressing a totality of feeling when instead I was tightly controlled within carefully constructed borders. Clinging desperately to the outer limits of an identity that I myself had imagined into existence, I saw that the implications were unending.

Dazed and nearly overcome, I responded, "I will try to commit myself to that, again."

And with that, the conversation approached its final closure. Had Swamiji been waiting all along for this energetic shift to happen? If so, he pretended not to notice.

"Much love, and as I say, feel free to call—and if I'm not in, leave a message."

"Okay, much love to you. And give my best to the Swamis."

"I will."

"Thank you, thank you." With that, I hung up, barely able to hold back the rush of many tears.

GREAT SWELLS OF love and release swept over and through me, and the weeping arrived without obstacles. Seana's magnificent life, our shared love, and her sudden death had initiated in me a cascading chain of sequences that felt unstoppable and powerful beyond anything I had ever imagined was possible.

Wave upon wave crested and crashed onto the shores of my old frame of understanding, dissolving obsolete ideas and memories. Instinctively, I knew that nothing else needed to happen, and I gave myself to it completely. That very thing that had crushed me, the disappearance of my beloved, had now become my guide.

Perhaps because it was so astonishing, I found it effortless. My mind and its chatter were erased. My heart was shattered, utterly and unconditionally heartbroken. But equally astounding to find was that it had been broken OPEN. Here and now, I was heartbroken—open. And love, supreme and matchless, was pouring from that red-hot fissure. Love for Seana, love for us, and a fathomless wellspring of gratitude for that rarest of opportunities to have shared these years together, learning side by side about what the poet, Mary Oliver, calls "this one wild and precious life."

It was one of Seana's favorite poems. The first time I came across "The Summer Day," a verse was hanging on her dining room wall inscribed in a piece of art. During our first weeks and months together, I remember reading it like a trail of breadcrumbs that might lead to some deeper insight into her core values.

Now, after twelve years together that had drawn from us our most radiant, as well as our shadow selves, I can only surmise that the beatific virtues which this poem is hinting at have no equivalent in language. Only being them comes close, and Seana embodied this poem every day for me. In so doing, she herself had been a signpost or encoded message from another realm. Like a clandestine invitation, the message was telling me that I would find something of inestimable value if I could but faithfully follow the trail back to its source inside.

Standing in the center of our tiny cottage paradise, awe-struck, a light rain began to fall. Gently, effortlessly, water was falling from the sky. Drops were bouncing and exploding into even tinier droplets, and then sliding through the cracks and gaps in the deck and merging with the gray sea below.

A velvety feeling of reverence enveloped me like a warm, soft blanket, and I understood that a presence, invisible but inconceivably real, had been calling to me for so long, reaching out through both the form and the formless nature of this one wild and precious life.

Who made the world?
Who made the swan, and the black bear?
Who made the grasshopper?
This grasshopper, I mean—
the one who has flung herself out of the grass,
the one who is eating sugar out of my hand,
who is moving her jaws back and forth instead of up and down—

who is gazing around with her enormous and complicated eyes.
Now she lifts her pale forearms and thoroughly washes her face.
Now she snaps her wings open, and floats away.
I don't know exactly what a prayer is.
I do know how to pay attention, how to fall down
into the grass, how to kneel down in the grass,
how to be idle and blessed, how to stroll through the fields,
which is what I have been doing all day.
Tell me, what else should I have done?
Doesn't everything die at last, and too soon?
Tell me, what is it you plan to do
with your one wild and precious life?

—Mary Oliver, "The Summer Day"

DAY THREE

8. Social Media

MONDAY MORNING, I awoke early and surveyed my immediate surroundings. Whatever lay behind me was done, and that which still had to happen certainly would, so I relaxed under the folds of our white down comforter and admired the woodland and ocean views from our bed. Better not to struggle when so much seems at stake and everything around you is whispering, *Slow down, listen, be here now.*

Swamiji's words had landed deep within my psyche, and an unmistakable shift was beginning to show itself like the tip of bright green when a seedling first breaks through soil.

Conjuring up my wife's beautiful, slender body, I reached out my hand into the empty space on the bed where her form would have been and caressed her head, stroked her brow, and spoke to her in my mind, recalling the deep pleasure she always experienced when I would take the time to wake with her.

I love you, Amore.

Our love is eternal.

Remember, we're here to learn deep trust. Well, here's our chance to take it to another level.

Be calm. Breathe with me.

Om Namah Shivaya on the inbreath, Om Namah Shivaya on the outbreath …

Let's open our hearts to the light. It's the light of your own Self. It's all of our true home.

It's where you and I will meet again.

Look for me there after this … There is a higher plan.

Say it with me, "There is a higher plan." It must be a beautiful, big plan to have this happen.

Trust. Let's learn trust together.

I trust what's happening with my whole heart. I trust.

Then, I began to sing to her. One of our favorite ways to entertain each other was to change the lyrics of a well-known song for our amusement. Ideally, this would make the other laugh as well as experience the pure delight of being the center of attention. This morning, however, our laughter was just a memory, and the only thing present was a deep love and respect for her.

Presently, the lyrics to "Volare" became, "Amore, oh oh. I love you, oh oh oh oh." Alone on the bed, it came out with a tenderness so genuine that it was as if I was laying it at her feet. This mournful little verse, a combination of playfulness and truth-telling in song, felt like the purest expression of what we loved about our lives together. Were she to be lying here next to me enjoying this spontaneous tribute of devotion, it would have been precious and memorable. That she was not, transformed it into an ode of the most exquisite melancholy.

Over and over, I crooned this melody for her with the

improvised phrasing. How rapturous and poignant such serious silliness was in every detail. Presently, a second verse was added: "Amore, oh oh. I love you, I think you know."

Just as the great black ocean and view of the evening sky had called up untold sorrow at its appointed time that first night, so did this simple improvisation of a 1950s Italian tune now sweep me up into the harsh light of bitter reality and the golden glow of immutable love.

Singing directly to Seana, I was telling her something so patently incontrovertible that I soon found myself plummeting through despair and out the other side. For as soon as I sang the words, "I love you, I think you know," I was entirely split open. Slipping through every substantially widening crack flowed intense love in the forms of ecstasy and agony. And to be completely transparent, it was the ecstasy that had the upper hand.

The melody hung in the air. No longer bound by time, the meaning of the words floated blissfully between us. It was as if we were sitting on the bed and gazing deeply into each other's eyes, whispering our devotion. Although the anguish of losing her was unrelenting, the pain of that separation was like an ultraviolet telescope. Aimed down through the roof of the cottage and directly onto the bed, it magnified our love a thousand-fold.

Baffled and blessed beyond measure, I kept singing it to her over and over. Somehow, out over the impassable abyss between us, verse and voice aloft, I was receiving far greater than I was giving. Yet, even immersed in such magnificence, I could not cross the dark brilliance of the divide. So for as long as I possibly could, I straddled the different realms. But eventually, it released me because unlike love, grief is not perfect.

WHEN I SAT for the Guru Gita later that morning, I could sense a certain energy building. My clear intention was to send Seana blessings. Needless to say, I had no idea whether or not she actually needed them. For all I knew, she was free and clear, and blissfully liberated from this world. Nonetheless, coursing through me was an unstoppable impulse, a river of longing to invoke a tremendous amount of grace, love, and light on her behalf.

This sacred chant begins by invoking the guru, both inner and outer—the spiritual teacher and link between the physical and the formless sacred inside the heart. It was something I had chanted many, many times over the years, and though it may sound strange to some, it had developed into a relationship that was twice as old and every bit as profound as the one I shared with my wife.

This morning, what mattered most was my trust in it, which over the years had grown deep and wide like a canyon. I knew it had immense power far beyond my own ability to comprehend. My intention was to unleash its full potential through the force of my love for Seana, like the stored kinetic energy in a snapping cable.

From its first metered lines, I gave myself up to that singular purpose and the protection that I believed it promised. This specific repetition of the chant, and there would be many more, was as much a laying down of arms as an invocation of blessings—an acknowledgment of my utter powerlessness in what was happening. After all, what else was left to me? What else was left to Seana?

In classical music, *development* is known to be the process by which an idea is communicated through its transformation and restatement. As the chant began to develop—beyond offering, I found myself pleading. My entire being became caught up in the fast-flowing river of this ancient prayer, and I was intent on willing it with all my might to bestow its full blessings upon my wife.

At approximately one hour in length and across the arc of its 182 verses, there were moments so full and heartrending that, for what seemed like minutes, I could not speak aloud the syllables or words for the tears and emotions surging through me. In arrhythmic cycles, a whole-body-ness of desolation would be followed by the most pristine love. A seemingly bottomless grief would well up only to eventually succumb, as if stalked by the gratitude that crushed it. Out of nowhere, a feeling of profound innocence would burst forth and radiate so powerfully that, like a cane field burned to the ground, nothing else remained. It was the most poignant lament I have ever known.

With a crescendo that cost me the last of my tissues, I sunk down effortlessly into the ensuing still point that had so evaded me earlier in this morning's meditation. How could something so traumatic also be equally ecstatic? Similar to my experience improvising "Volare" this morning, it genuinely mystified me. And not for the last time I wondered if, close at hand or buried somewhere in lush, dark stillness—there might be a hidden message, an inscrutable and resonant seed of an idea whose melodic, developing theme was meant just for me.

LATER THAT AFTERNOON, after a walk along winding, gently sloped forest trails in the woods behind our property and among giant, one hundred-year-old trees, I began to feel noticeably more clear-headed. To become extricated, even slightly, from the cramped, pressurized sensations that—like a silky cocoon or a spider's web (depending upon one's point of view)— had enveloped me since Saturday afternoon was surprisingly revitalizing.

The filtering sunlight, the scent of pine, and the soft, muted sounds down on the forest floor all combined to usher in the unhurried restoration of inner balance. Wandering among the tall trees was like having forest guardians around me on all sides, and had much the same effect as encouragements being whispered in my ear. For two days, I had been looking inward, so to now look out and up, straight up, and see the domed, blue sky between swaying trees a hundred feet overhead not only stretched my neck but my mind and spirits as well.

THERE WERE OTHER things on my to-do list today in addition to grieving. A new balance between the inner and outer world began to take shape in the form of a call from the Boulder County Coroner. Since I did not pick up the call, but merely watched it ring through, identify its caller, and leave me a voicemail, I now had both a visual and aural reminder of Seana's lifeless body. Though she was long gone from it, her corpse was a physical representation of all that I was not yet ready to contemplate, let alone see or touch.

I noticed the discomfort and impulsive desire to immediately call back and tell them to do the cremation as soon as possible— to burn that hollow shell to ashes. Yet, it was also like an annoying dog barking in the background of my mind. It cautioned me against rejecting the unexamined. Wasn't this the very vehicle that had served and protected my beloved? Why wouldn't I be willing to see and honor it one last time?

When I finally called the coroner's office back, I found on the other end a compassionate, gentle woman who shared as many details as possible after only forty-eight hours. She informed me of the things I would need to address quite soon, and I learned new information too.

The accident occurred in Boulder County at the intersection of Highway 66 and Sixty-sixth Street around 10:00 a.m. on a dry, sunny morning. I knew this highway well, for Seana and I had begun to establish our relationship in earnest near that particular area of Boulder. It is a rural highway that we often traveled on our way to hike Rabbit Mountain, which is located less than a mile further down the road from that very intersection.

Driver Number One was in his brand-new Jeep Cherokee and had showed no signs of drinking or texting. Witnesses had seen his car inexplicably come across the middle divide, enter Seana's lane, and strike our Prius head-on, crushing it several feet inward. It spun around and was propelled across the oncoming lane until it collided into a tree where it came to rest in a small gully. Seana had been taken to the emergency where they unsuccessfully tried to revive her. Preliminary autopsy examination showed that she died of blunt force trauma to the head and body, and cardiac arrest.

THE NIGHT OF Seana's accident, in addition to Sharon, I had sent off a text to my closest friend in the world other than my wife. As might be expected, it was short and to the point.

"I need you to chant the Guru Gita and share with friends. I cannot. Seana was killed in a car accident today in CO."

John was someone I had known since first moving to Hawaii in the mid-1990s—one of the most genuinely compassionate and light-hearted human beings you will ever meet. Although we were the same age, John had been practicing Siddha Yoga even longer than I had. He was the person whom Seana and I had chosen to marry us ten years before on the same sandy beach on Oahu where we first met under a June full moon.

Perhaps as a reflex of walking in the woods, of looking forward and not back, it felt like it was time to reach out to John. Though I had fled into solitude and silence and was still in retreat, a willingness was slowly emerging to look outward and upward once again.

John picked up the call after the first ring. Before I could even say hello, he was on the line.

"Hey, buddy, how are you doing?"

In his voice, I could hear his concern and heaviness of heart as clearly as if he were greeting me after a return from a disastrous tour of duty.

"I'm hanging in there. Doing the practices pretty much all day and waking up at 3:00 a.m. every night."

"Well, that's good, that's good. Meditation will support you to get through this."

"It's actually chanting that's the most helpful. The Guru Gita, the mantra, Evening Arati ... it's all I'm doing, really." While this wasn't precisely true, it was shorthand for "I'm alright and doing the most beneficial actions possible every day."

"Good, good." He was still feeling me out, proceeding tentatively. "You have a lot of people concerned out here. A lot of people really love you, you know? You have a lot to live for still."

Message received. He wants to know if I'm suicidal.

"I know. Thank you. No one needs to worry about me. Please tell them I'm fine."

I could not help but chuckle, however sadly. "Actually, it's really weird, you know? Sometimes there's so much love and bliss that I can't tell what's going on anymore. Like ... is this a tragedy or a gift? I know that sounds strange."

"No, no. You have to go through it. You have to let yourself feel it. It's just that people really need to hear from you. They need to know that you're all right. They're worried about you."

I had forgotten that others might be concerned about me. Actually, I had given zero thought to how others might be doing. The two towers, death—all-consuming, and love—all-embracing, had monopolized every facet of my awareness and would continue to do so for quite some time.

"People are posting on social media amazing tributes to Seana," he continued. "I'm learning things about her that I had no idea she did in her life. I'm completely in tears as I read them, and I don't even know who these people are! But they need to hear from you. They want to know how you are."

"Okay, I understand. I will. I spoke to Swamiji yesterday and he reminded me about the significance of her thirteenth day and sending her into the light, so maybe I can post something inviting people to join me in sending love and light to Seana on that day. And I can also let them know I'm alright, but still need my privacy. I need this time to myself. It's so unbelievably precious—and surprising!"

"Yeah, of course it is, buddy. That's great. So, then maybe just write a little bit about, you know, something that says you're okay, and that they can help send Seana to the light on her thirteenth day. Then just ask everyone to respect your privacy."

"Okay, I can do that."

"Do you know anything about the guy that caused the accident?"

"No, just that he crossed the middle line and hit her head-on. There is no evidence of alcohol or drugs."

"Was he texting?"

"They don't think so. The officers checked his phone right afterwards. But this is not about him, John. Seana's death is way bigger and beyond one person being at fault or to blame. That's not the approach I'm taking."

"Very good. I agree. Seana's life was much bigger than that. So, maybe you want to share that with them too. Some of the posts out there are ... there are people who are really angry and blaming him, lashing out at the world."

"No, I don't want that! And Seana would never want that, either."

"Right, I know. So, you need to tell them. Steer them in another direction, the direction that you *do* want."

AFTER WE HUNG up, I sat there a while in thought, already imagining what I might say. Not wanting to keep the company of anyone but Seana, my solitude had also removed me from whatever reaction to her death was happening out in the world.

Later, when I finally logged on and began to read what her friends, colleagues, and past students were posting, it was as if I had stumbled out from a dark cave into a dazzling, sunlit afternoon. The sudden glare was blinding, but the warmth and light emanating from their words were wildly beautiful and life-resuscitating. I was definitely not alone.

It seemed many of the same emotions that had been violently surging through me were also present in their minds and hearts and scattered brilliantly like stars. It was as if everyone had at last looked up. Or were we all looking up together, because where else is there to look? Where can such rare beauty as that one be found? Where does light go when it disappears from view?

I also noticed a few of the threads venting an overwhelming sadness, frustration, and anger, assigning all guilt and liability to the driver, to all drivers—to texting, drinking, and to any force that would remove someone who was so obviously, materially, and fundamentally making a positive difference in the world.

Yet, from what I could see, Seana's divine radiance dominated the online conversations. As in life, so in death—Seana brought out your very best. When you were with her, and especially if you were blessed to be in her presence for any length of time, beguiling worlds of possibility would begin to orbit your thought processes as if conjured by spirits. She called to qualities within you that, as yet, may not even exist but in her mind were there all along just waiting to be summoned.

And I learned about Seana, too. I began to understand even more clearly why it was that everywhere we went, people seemed to gravitate to her, to love and respect her without hesitation. With Seana, there was not the usual waiting period for most before they would intuitively trust her. Vibrantly alive and extraordinarily beautiful, she exuded a humility and genuine interest in others that is rare and almost unheard of in this peculiar era of round-the-clock celebrated self-absorption.

Erratically but inevitably, a deluge of mind-blowing testimonials was popping up everywhere online like corks after a heavy storm. One after another, they appeared in vivid, cathartic, and inspired essays of such longing and devotional gratitude for her presence in their lives that it was clear the authors, too, were as changed by Seana in death as they had been in life.

Reading their words, it felt as if I had been granted access to someone's secret and confidential diary. If I wished, it seemed that I had to only lower my gaze to catch a glimpse of the pools of tears that must be gathered like raindrops or priceless diamonds all around their papers, pens, pencils, and computers.

One former student wrote of a hike they had taken at a dark time in her life when she felt trapped in a job that was crushing her spirit and mental health. After hearing about it, Seana had refused to climb back down the mountain that they had ascended until the young woman agreed to call that instant and give them her two-week's notice because she could not continue in something that was what Seana called "so profoundly life-taking."

Online, a groundswell of public mourning was gathering. It was stunning to learn how many people attributed their single-most significant breakthrough in life to a specific interaction with Seana, or to the INVST community program at CU Boulder that she had taken charge of while still in her twenties as program director and strapped to her wings. So that, like sudden upward flight to a prairie dog, it came to represent for undergrads what was unheard of in a university setting: a pathway and map to a meaningful and inspired life of extraordinary possibility.

9. INVST

A T AROUND THE six-month mark in my relationship with Seana, I remember being present at a graduation of her INVST students at the CU Boulder campus. Not knowing what to expect, and therefore full of presumptions in spite of myself, I imagined exiting the auditorium two or three hours later having listened to long recitations, lists of accomplishments, and perfunctory anecdotes from early-twenty-somethings.

Instead, I departed that chamber in awe and deeply restored. For these were not stiff and lifeless monologues, not a shallow looking back in coy modesty, but rather a forward-looking vision of beauty and greatness replete with declarations of deep and inspired commitment to living uncommon lives.

From the first graduate to the last, it was like being inhaled into a deep pool of light where hours passed in brilliant flashes. I sat in rapt attention, repeatedly moved and educated by young lives already altered by deep insights and shaken awake with intuitions of the profound metamorphosis inherent in all life. This was delivered to my ears by fresh faces who seemed almost delirious with a rare and increasingly elusive grade of authentic, heartfelt gratitude. And according to them, it was all due to the last two years of their lives in the INVST program, and above all, always above all, it was because of Seana.

Afterwards, parents, students, and friends paid their respects to her and then scattered in every direction, zigzagging away in curlicues of intimacy like sparks from a chimney.

At last, Seana and I were alone and strolling under campus trees. The canopies shimmered and danced above us in a thousand shades of green and yellow. It was like being sheltered beneath great umbrellas of color, light, and sound.

Though we walked side-by-side, I rarely looked at her directly unless we were conversing. A heavenly silence seemed to be swirling between and around us while all our forward motion felt rimmed in stillness. Filled to the brim with Seana and by her students' beauty and promise, I floated beside her form as if in orbit around it. Our stroll even had its own soundtrack in the ambient sounds of leaves twirling, the far-off murmurs of families laughing and breathing in harmony and contentment, and the wind rising and falling as it recited what could only be secret poems and mantras held in reserve for just such initiations.

The outer scene gave the impression of peering through a soft-focus lens where all the footpaths, knolls, and trees swayed in approval. Perhaps a sphere of light forms around all souls when they are falling deeply in love, for my brain was awash with what felt like blurry recognition of this moment and of her. It was as if subatomic particles were colliding at light speed like ecstatic drunkards and leaving trails of luminescence in their wake. And though we occasionally intersected with others along the path, it felt like we were the only ones in existence—two congruent points wandering side by side, encased within our protected bubble.

Enchantingly, the voices of graduates and their relations strolling by seemed distant, bouncing off the invisible shell around us.

The conversations penetrated just enough so that their exchanges and expressions of love intermingled with us but were wonderfully muted. In this way, neither the meaning of their words, which was meant just for them, nor an awareness of others intruded into our sphere.

Still unsure how to proceed with her, I also felt myself teetering on an edge. From every direction splendid reverberations of the many graduations seemed to all be converging in waves, and then spreading outward again like the ripples of a lake. Looking across the campus, blue-green panoramas rose and ebbed as we passed among them like gently rolling swells in an open ocean— whereas in my mind, hesitation and recklessness cavorted back and forth as if a child were playing with a light switch.

Was I excited? Certainly I was, but apprehensive, too. The moment seemed so very delicate. What if I should interrupt the merging that had mysteriously begun during the graduation ceremony and, for all I knew, might still be happening? Or maybe this moment felt tenuous because I was so terribly afraid that only I might be feeling the delirium of union, and her radiant beauty was beyond my reach, for certainly everyone present in that auditorium must be madly in love with her now.

A metered cadence, hypnotic and irresistible, carried us forward in perfect counterpoint. Tethered to the soft rhythm of our footsteps, I was aware that, as long as we were together, there was hope. So familiar was this and she that it gave the impression of being age-old, as if it was a reenactment of something we had shared many times before.

But all that was just an intuition. To reach out to her I would have to summon the courage I needed to find a way to speak the truth and then vow to live by it for the rest of this life—but it meant exposing what I had been vigilantly protecting since boyhood: inviolable intimacy. However, if I intended to continue down this path, there was simply no avoiding it. Nor would there be any future with Seana that I would be able to sustain. But I feared that I had not yet done that work. Thus, alongside the desire churning within me was a tangible foreboding and dread that I hoped would remain imperceptible to her.

It made complete sense. Hadn't I witnessed first-hand the carnage that an unhappy marriage has the power to inflict? How abuse can devastate a family from within until darkness and fear reside in every corner of the house—and still, you and everyone you love must return to live and sleep in that house? And while I was not my mother, and I certainly was not her second husband, no other blueprint had been so vividly burned into my memory.

Walking by Seana's side, I had a premonition that her presence was hypnotizing me like a magic spell that could not be undone. The moment was demanding that I lean out even further over this abyss, and with that I saw my great fear. It was of surrender, of losing myself, and the alarming necessity of accepting that possibility.

Sweet deliverance arrived in the form of sound. Foreshadowing our future, Seana's resplendent voice came to get me where I had curled up deep within.

Turning to look at me, she asked, "So, what did you think?"

I hesitated, hoping to communicate something beautiful and miraculous, something close to the sum of the shock and reverence I was feeling for what the afternoon had provided. Although I hoped and suspected we were already deeply in love, we did not yet know one another perfectly, and I found myself confounded, wanting to convey to her so many things at once—what the ceremony had meant to me and what I thought it might have meant to the students and families; that I was stunned, inspired, and a little unnerved by what I had witnessed; that I was completely mesmerized by her brilliance and beauty; and that I knew her students loved her and claimed her for their champion. But mostly, I wanted her to know what it had taught me about her soul, and I had no words for that.

Finally, speechless and at a low tide when high tide was needed, I could only smile and meet her gaze in shy admiration and a poorly concealed infatuation. All hope at making some kind of impression I renounced as impossible, for the goddess who accompanied me was dazzling, luminous, and unmatched—and I knew this as I knew my name.

Gradually, it dawned on me that I should simply share with her the one word that had been springing forth within my mind like divine fragrance since somewhere around the midpoint of the graduation ceremony. Though Seana would not have known it at that point in our relationship, it was the highest compliment I could have spoken. Nor could I have known that speaking it here and now would marry and fuse our love beyond my wildest imagination. But, over time, it was to become the best and most accurate description of our union.

"Sacred. It felt sacred, Seana."

In the Hawaiian language, *ohana* is an ancient and enlightened idea of family that expands outward beyond the limitation of blood relatives to embrace others within a broader sense of community. It has a respect for our fellow humanity that, depending upon with whom you speak, is either in the process of disappearing or already long gone among the *haoles* on the mainland of the United States. No matter. For it is alive and well in the Hawaiian Islands, and has been for thousands of years.

My new online ohana, the growing family that was now

beginning to share on social media their most intimate feelings of devastation, needed to be acknowledged and enfolded. At least for a few weeks, we had something profound and beautiful in common and were already bound by it—the sense of a great love lost.

Sitting down to write to them on social media, I felt a new purpose and focus, and it was no longer *me*. It was time to serve Seana, to thank her as best I could for all that she had come to mean to me. This was the crux of the shift; *my* grief, *my* pain, *my* heartbreak. My heart was no longer in it. And this pivot, from *me and mine* to her, somehow changed everything.

This first communication needed to be short and to the point, letting them know that I was all right as well as inviting them to join together in visualizing Seana rising into the light on her thirteenth day.

Surprisingly, the words came forth in quick bunches, my heart speaking fluently and freely as it does among ohana. Therefore, it did not take long to write and share with them, connected as we were by her light that was now at its strongest, even as it was fading.

10. Awake and Livid

I AWAKEN IN the middle of the night, again. This is the third consecutive night, and I do not fight it nor make any attempt to fall back asleep. It's impossible. Rather, I get up and move in the direction the previous sleepless nights have pointed me—toward the meditation cushion.

But tonight, something is off. When I sit down, rhythmically breathing in and out several times to initiate meditation, again, the most peculiar feeling arises inside me and will not allow my body or mind to access stillness. So, I shift my approach and attempt to ease into it by chanting the mantra for a while, but it's as if something unseen is bubbling up to interfere. It's unsettling, and neither meditation nor chanting will soothe this odd sensation.

Looking out across the water to Maury Island, there are no lights on anywhere at 3:00 a.m. The cottage is swathed in stillness and feels soft and warm like the black cashmere scarf handed down to me from my grandfather. How wonderful and strange to feel him close tonight, that saintly man, long since dissolved yet subtly present. It's a good omen.

Outside, the deep blackness of the night softly hums. Its

vibrations are as soothing as a baby's inhalation and exhalation, yet returning to bed is not an option.

Wide awake and sitting in the dark, a benevolent bright lantern of a moon has been lit and eventually glides downward to perch on top of a brilliant, sparkling column in the black water. The moon is now in two places at once, up above and down below, and this seems to fit well with my own inner state.

Split between the outer world's reflection in the perfectly flat mirror of the water, smooth as glass, and the vivid memories in my mind, I am unable to reconcile the two worlds. Thusly divided, I watch them both, just as I am vigilantly watching for signs of the one I love in the throbbing pulsations flickering overhead, opening and closing, coupling and uncoupling in infinity of starlight.

Starlight, with her trillion eyes all twinkling and winking their delight at such a night as this, is singing and running across the blackness of the night sky. And, like an only child, she does so rhythmically, incessantly, as if eager to show off her infinite storehouse, her generosity, and her precocious talents. Her glittering lights never tire of making every effort to convey the greater arc of a just balance that only the cosmos seems capable of exhibiting with any consistency. Such playfulness and innocence exist within the gaze of that wild child, utterly free and unself-conscious, and one gracious glance of hers seems supremely capable of restoring equilibrium in the world.

And so I listen, head turned upward, and stare so long that in due time I find myself looking not only heavenward, but inward too. Death cannot mar eternity, and the universe knows this, which, of course, is why it is so astonishingly beautiful.

As if I had been aimlessly sleepwalking, the symmetry of the outer world and its loveliness return my thoughts quite naturally to Seana, and I begin to wonder about her. Might tonight's restlessness be a signal from her? Is there something she wants to say to me?

As soon as I have that thought, a hush envelops the room so noticeably that my mind instantly pivots from talking to listening. There, in the lull, I ask wordlessly, *Is there something you want to tell me, Amore?* Suspending all thoughts, my concentration narrows to the point of a pin.

Instantly appearing in my mind as a single, isolated thought is, *Why did this have to happen now?*

Instinctively, I grab the yellow spiral binder from the table that I had left there for the journaling that did not come, and write in huge letters across the top of the page:

AMORE, I AM LISTENING

"Why did this have to happen now?"

Inside my head, I see it and hear it in unison. Amazed and startled, yet immediately written down, I know them to be her words.

"Everything was literally falling into place with ease."

Word by word, fitfully, an entire sentence just appeared out of nothing. Then, one after another, herky-jerky—and as long as my own words and thoughts are not paid any attention, hers spring forth in a disjointed but steady chain where each one disappears before the next one materializes.

"Antioch University, *the* job I'd been most wanting, made for me. I had deeply connected to being teacher again with the Natural Hazards staff in Boulder. I was making a difference. Ecstatic, rave reviews of the process I led them through. You and I have arrived into such ease and partnership!"

Out of impenetrable darkness, her words are materializing in pulsing bursts of vocabulary at the center of my mind. In something that is a cross between a sonorous dictionary and a roulette wheel, a random letter emerges as an inner sound, followed by a pause, and then the leading consonant or vowel chooses the word. The key to receptivity and accuracy seems to be to stay out of it altogether.

"I *love* being Mrs. Steffen, being Seana Lowe Steffen, being Seana Steffen. I was feeling your body, your touch, your gaze, knowing you're a call away and I can talk with you about anything. Why? Why now? You are the love of my lifetime. Why must we be separated when we know that—love being that together?

"Better together. Life *is* better together. So then, why now? We'd worked so hard, you had worked *so* hard! *Tapasya!* Colitis! Your mother! Your sisters! Your family not accepting me, embracing me. Why did they do that?"

Her question punctures me as unmistakably as if she had taken a pin to a balloon. That was a wrong that was never made right, and in my mind I hear myself wondering, *Should I ask them why?*

"Yes, please *do* ask them," comes her immediate reply.

Filled with remorse for my beloved and regret for my family, I ache for both. Once noble, a magnificent lighthouse for so many in our community, my two sisters and mother should have been among the greatest gifts I had to share with my wife. But our family could not hold the bright promise of its early years, and instead festered. Inclined to self-important judgments and fault-finding, the women in my family feared Seana's independence, and mine too, and from the outset opposed and maligned her.

Here, within the cottage and my mind, Seana is in the room and speaking directly to me, through me. If it is not already glaringly obvious, the naked truthfulness of it certainly is. By dawn, any doubts I may have furtively harbored about the source will have long since vanished like tiny ships in a cyclone.

"I'm *mad*! I'm *sad*! I'm so terribly sad …

"It feels like depression, the deep hole. Please, no more Lord of the Rings—Ringwraiths, Nazgul— no more Frodo."

I can feel her sliding downward on slippery slopes and away from me.

Half speaking to herself, she murmurs, "You helped me leave these behind. What happens now? I need you to talk to, to calm me down. And look, you're writing. Yes, you're listening, but what then? You and I can't do this for each other anymore!"

This is gut-wrenching to witness. Any illusions I was clinging to that upon death she had simply floated blissfully up, or in, or away, have been shattered into a thousand shards and replaced by a fearful apprehension for her well-being that shakes me mercilessly to my core.

One of the handful of physical challenges Seana faced while in a body was a genetic risk of depression. Because she was such a radiant, highly accomplished life force in the world, very few people knew that she had received sporadic professional and medicinal support for this. But hearing her bring up her warning signals, I shudder at the implications.

On the line below hers, I scribble, "I am listening, my beautiful Amore. I am here for you. I will ask my Gurumayi how I can always be here for you when you need. What else should I say or ask her?"

"Tell her how sad I am, and mad, and confused. I *love* life. I love life with you, my beloved, my Earl—I have nothing now. What will I do without my Earl? You are my protector. Who will protect me when you're gone?"

She sounds dazed, pulled and stretched like taffy. The empty space within my mind appears and disappears as if lit by a strobe light. Each word arrives alone, or in twos and threes, unthought and unplanned. On this silent runway, she drops words that land here and there and occasionally in clusters like clumped grapes. The focus required to stay receptive to them is unambiguous, distinct, and blunt as a hammer. Thoughts are allowed, just not mine.

She continues, as if speaking directly to my teacher, Gurumayi.

"Why didn't you do what Barron said you would—protect us from calamity? This is *the* biggest calamity. If you are who you say you are, help us—help me. Help me understand. How is *this* ease?"

Then I feel her drifting away again, and she finally asks, "Why do little children get murdered or die? They are innocent!

"I did *nothing* wrong but love my husband, my planet, every living creature. I wanted to help—to serve. *that's all I ever asked to do*—to be of service to those in need. Why couldn't I have been allowed to do that in love and for love—happy, truly happy?"

It's as if she is drowning and I am only a few feet away, unable to catch hold of her. Despair is setting in, and I can feel it. She is struggling and thrashing wildly, exhausting herself. I focus hard on taking it all, devouring and listening to every fear while staying as near as I can so she knows that she is not alone. But though no further away than a thought in my head, she is hopelessly beyond my reach.

"I was finally happy. I felt optimism, joy, elation, ecstasy. Why did it get taken away? What *is* your plan? Why is grace, and plan, concealed like *Shiva Nataraja's* arm?

"I was just coming to know happiness for the first time in my life, and you snatched it away from me. What have I done to deserve that? Did I not have what Barron calls, merit? I lived purely, with constant attention to the shakti, honoring her in so many ways daily—every day. Not a day passed without my honoring and praying to Mother Shakti to make me her instrument, to make me a voice for those unheard. *That's all I ever asked for.*

"Even when Barron was in the ashram and asked me for my prayer to Nityananda for burning, it took *him* prodding me to move even a tiny bit away from just saying what *I truly wanted and still want. I want to make a difference. I want to love my husband, Barron Steffen, and be loved by him, touched and caressed by him.*"

Perhaps it is purely because I am tuned in and listening to her for the first time since her accident and, at last unleashed, her pent-up anguish is rushing through the opening. Yet, it is entirely conceivable, bona fide, that tonight's volcanic eruption is happening because it was not just for Seana to endure, afraid and alone, but also mine to share with her.

"Why didn't you make him touch me more, kiss me more, love on me more? He became an ascetic after he *got me.* I needed his physical affection, and I got a monk. Why wasn't he a monk instead? It hurt, and it hurts.

"You should have told him—*with words*—to love me more. Did you not know? Why didn't you tell Barron to express his love for me more fully, daily … plan for it like he planned to meditate and go to the ashram? You were *always* his first choice. I didn't get what he advertised to be—a lover. Someone who is able to physically love another human being."

Inside me, a glowing hot coal of an ember, long smoldering, ignites into flames. I feel her reproach and the hot sting of remorse within my body, so that the mounting desolation and lucent fever of her suffering is not just heartbreaking and unnerving, but also closer to me than my own breath. Having heard these indictments before and knowing their veracity, it gashes me—a long blade twisting in the old wounds. How paradoxical and strange to have this experience originating from within my own mind.

Nevertheless, avoiding nothing, imbibing each nuance like soil absorbing every droplet of rain, I let nothing pass unexamined.

"Yes, think about it, Barron. *Please*. Before you go and do it to someone else. I see your doubt, your fear of choosing another woman—a Siddha Yogini this time, so you can pranam together at your Gurumayi's feet, live in her ashram, have children that serve and grow up with her. Like Sara, right? Are they happy, James and his wife? Are they happier than we were—than we were about to be—when I got my *dream* job and you were finally getting paid your worth?

"And in one swoop, it is all dust. Gone. No chance to change or be recovered. No tapasya, no chanting, meditating, or ashram summer visits can bring me back into life, into my husband's arms."

She is livid, all at once urgent and near, suffocating and welcome, a speculum of intimacy that I could not have dreamed. Bitter outrage is pouring out, and it's not just because she feels like pristine opportunities for happiness have been stolen from her. Nor is it that her longing to love fully, which is as genuine and natural to her as humility to a venerable sage, has gone unfulfilled. It is, instead, that she had dedicated this lifetime to the selfless service of all living things as her chosen vehicle for expressing that love ever more perfectly, and this was the very thing that had been snatched away.

"Gurumayi, Barron says you are Love. You are God. Is God so cruel? If that is Siddha Yoga, I want *no* part of it. If this is your Big Plan, I don't like it—don't understand it.

"I miss the love. I miss my husband. I miss my planet ... walking in nature as my muse. I miss sunshine on water. I miss the rain, gray days, the water color in Shark's Cove, and knowing my husband is waiting for me."

A silence follows. Had she been curled up before me in a heap,

I would have liked to brush the soft golden hair from her forehead and kiss her softly. I would have liked to shape labyrinthine patterns with those gentle kisses, so that they would drift about her exquisite face like a tempest gathering strength before making landfall.

"The pain and ecstasy of separation? That's Divine Love? Masochism. Male-generated suffering. Gurumayi, all I wanted was Ease. *Arama*. All I asked for was prosperity with ease, and look what I got. I lost the love of my life. And I lost the work that I am passionate about, another true love."

My beloved is in full fury now, and just as she was in life, she is unstoppable. So much of what Seana is railing against are pieces of our past showing up in the present. *Incompletes* is the word she often used to describe them, and now they were karmic driftwood clogging the river.

"So I am asking you, Gurumayi. Please help me understand. I have no peace. And I need peace or I will die, endlessly, losing all I love—I've lost it *all*.

"I'm so sad. I'm so tired. I want to just give up ... give in. I've done my very best.

"I put forth all the self-effort I could, even in the face of so little grace in return ... the two wings of the bird ... why is that wing broken? I don't understand."

Bereft and exhausted, she stalls as if resting between the two wings of a bird. The two wings, self-effort and grace, that together are said to be capable of lifting a soul above the fray of the world, upward and beyond the reach of thoughts and desires to where lasting attainments abide in silence.

"Please, help me. If you can help me, please help me *now*. Please help me, Gurumayi. Please help me, Baba. And anyone else listening, if you hear me and can feel me, I—*need—help—right—now*. Not the thirteenth day. *Now*. Om Namah Shivaya!

"I can't do it on my own anymore. You took Barron. The *one* thing that helped me the most. Please give me something—some of your grace. I'm so, so tired."

Hearing her cry out in desperation utterly pierces me, and my mind collapses into a point of singularity where time is stopped and nothing else exists. There is only this present moment and purpose, now and forever—and were it possible, I would have wagered my life on it as Seana had hers.

From within me, a dark and timeless void opens up with a blinding, violent implosion that is a summons of intention and willpower unlike any I have ever known before or since. It is as if ripples, instead of emanating outward from the original point of disturbance, reverse back inward and all arrive simultaneously at the center where, upon arrival, like an atomic bomb, the explosion creates a mushroom cloud reaching up into the sky. And—not yet done but rather still gathering strength in the pause at its apex— turns and looks down on its target and locks in with deadly certainty. And only then does it begin its free fall downward from the height of the heavens.

Gravity, knowing what is being attempted and deeply moved, adds its support to the descent of this nascent power. Emboldened and whipped into a frenzy, it is returning to earth holding before it the sum of its life, the mass of all its good and pure actions, like the tip of a weapon. Now knowing its purpose for being born, it is no longer troubled about life or death, but only that her suffering, the bullseye that must be annihilated, shall never return to her.

That was how the gathering of my inner power felt.

And so, like a general committing all his assets to one battle, I scrawl across the page in huge letters:

I AM SENDING EVERYONE FOR YOU, AMORE.

IF I HAVE ANY GRACE ACCUMULATED OR LOVE FROM YOU

MY GURUS, MY SIDDHAS,

PLEASE—HELP—SEANA—NOW.

GO TO HER NOW.

DON'T LET HER SUFFER ANOTHER INSTANT.

11. In a Place That Is Not a Place

IN A PLACE that is not a place at all, but a circumference of light, we voyaged around the farthest side of the dark ellipse and returned again, changed. Those pre-dawn hours were a blast furnace, a forge where impurities liquefy. Once molten, they are consumed by fire and washed away. This, too, seems right, aligned, and congruent with the bell curve of our relationship—from its first green bud at the convergence of blue ocean, sand, and domed sky—through years and layers of back-to-back-to-back challenges burned through like parched kindling, all of it leading to tonight's fireworks.

Dawn is nearing, and in the serenity and silence that remains like the deep and dreamless sleep after a great battle, small hints of silver light creep into the seams of the darkness outside the cottage. The sun, still nestled out of sight, is burning with pleasure. There is nothing more to give or say tonight. Nor is anything left of me but a few glowing embers, and I love her more than I ever have.

It may be that tonight's events were confirmation of my shared *dharma*, my sacred duty, or a consequence for the prior absence of it, but it is clear that nothing is ever missed. Whether in life or after it, no thought, word, or action—conscious or latent—goes unrecorded by that luminous flame of the Self within. Accordingly, tonight we added one more magnificent gem to an epic story that rips away veils of illusions like toys from the hands of stubborn children.

How inscrutable and ruthless is grace, the other wing of the bird that no one can catch or force to do their bidding. Our self-effort draws grace, but never ever will command it. Yet it allows us to ride freely if we can balance between both wings.

Seana was right to question grace tonight. Not because that could ever alter its divine, enigmatic plans but if only to remain awake and vigilant to what matters most, like a heliotropic blossom constantly turning its face upward and sideways to track the bright path of the sun. I am in awe of her sublime bravery, her ethereal effort. How courageous of her, even in the face of darkness and death, to continue her questioning, seeking first to understand how to ever more deeply trust what she often referred to as "the long view."

And I think that must be at least one of any number of unearthly purposes for this brutal, titanic event—taking the long view of a much greater arc. That arc will never defer. Already it is ushering her on ahead to a forgotten world that is, quite possibly, even more real than the one she is departing. And like an arrow flying out straight and clearing this one single life's narrow trajectory, it traces a path parallel to the incorruptible and divine obligation we all have upon leaving the physical body to keep flowing onward.

Though beyond my capacity to fully understand, it seems to me that the purpose of Seana's life, that wish to be of service and remove suffering from the world, is so pure and flawless that it cannot simply be extinguished along with the physical body.

Something so universal in nature must carry over from form into formless existence.

Like an empyrean Venn diagram that includes all the contrasting and contradicting rings within it, intersecting every dimension and realm of possibility, or like the infinitesimal point in time and space when the tide crests and, having gone out as far as it can, begins its return—in the same way—compassion, goodness, kindness, and humility—these are not things. And, therefore, once learned and assimilated, they cannot be killed.

For, unlike the enchanting beauty of Seana's breathtaking form, love is timeless. She has been here before, and will return. Tonight is like that limitless space that exists just after the exhale but before inhaling again—or when we close our eyes, open them, and then close them once again. Who knows for certain which one is the enduring reality?

For the next hour, dawn is advancing. Golden, feathery wings unfold in ribbons of flamelike colors above the cottage and rage below in the Salish Sea, and I am about to become engrossed in writing down a laundry list of prayers and blessings to accompany her on her journey. Each one begins with "May she," as in, "May she know the answers to all her questions; May she know peace that surpasses all understanding; May she be shown the love of God and the heart of Siddha Yoga..."

I take solace in the possibility that these will assuage any turbulence as she rides upon silver-blue slipstreams while winding through wormholes amid as yet unnamed colors of living light. Perhaps out there beyond ideas of wrongdoing and rightdoing, in that field Rumi told me about what seems like a thousand years ago, she will recognize it as our true home and lie down in the grass.

Or, even more deliciously, it might be that when she finally alights onto whatever translucent subtle realm that, even now, she is being silently drawn toward, these blessings that I am sending will have already arrived to greet her homecoming like birthday cards.

But, before I turn to begin that list, I hear one last thing from her in my head.

"And I miss my cat!"

Day Four

12. Guru Gita

AFTER A LATE-morning nap and breakfast, I awaken feeling significantly lighter and somehow cleaner. Deeply blessed, even. This was not how I had expected it to go. Seana's sudden reappearance last night was a game changer.

In its aftermath, to continue clinging to preconceptions that were obviously inaccurate not only seems ignorant, but as foolish as if I was trying to climb a tall tree while holding onto objects in both hands—counterproductive to both task and purpose. Thus, since dawn, any remaining presumptions of what I should expect from this process have begun to evaporate away like sparkling trails of mist in the hot sun.

Word must be spreading because I have many more texts and voicemails on my phone this morning. Silently, I thank the names of those who sent them, and notice that even my dear friends in Italy have learned of it. Many years ago, I lived in Milan as a young musician and fell in love with it and them. That period in Europe was like the foreshadowing of a much deeper awakening, for the Italians taught me the sweetness of sharing together the simple delight of being alive and exuded a mischievous playfulness that was like a revelation at the time.

Reading through all the texts at once has a cumulative effect on me, and by the time I reach the final one from one of my closest Italian friends whom I have not heard from in many years, I am openly weeping.

How many hidden caves of the heart must exist that we have no knowledge of? Just when I was sure that my grief had emptied all its chambers last night like a pistol in a brawl, here was another. As if out of nowhere, platoons of thunderclouds suddenly roll through our tiny kitchen. They pour in rain like little soldiers through the gaps between the fingers covering my face—drenching and shaking the table, stool, and floor with my sobs.

From this, a powerful urge arises to share this boundless sweetness with my extended ohana, that family who by virtue of the heart is beyond blood. I long to let them know how moved I am by their words. *Although it may appear as if I am unreachable right now, you are here with me!*

Turning instinctively to my journal, I grab my pencil and compose a love letter to them, and post it online later that morning.

> *I heard from a dear friend today. Yes, it was you*
> *who touched my heart and caused these tears to flow*
> *again—these sobs to rattle my being top to bottom. I*
> *lost my Seana, my wife, I think you know. And your*
> *thoughtful texts and posts—the evident, tangible signs*
> *of love for me and my Amore—are helping in ways*
> *I never imagined I could need. From all that I am, I*

thank you. I wish you endless blessings for such selfless
kindness. Because it was you, speaking for my beloved,
to comfort me and remind me that I am not alone and
that she is not alone.

AS THE TIME to offer the morning Guru Gita approached, I sensed a narrowing of my thoughts and a gathering fullness of intention and energy that augured an auspicious event. After revisiting the many pages in my journal that had resulted from the previous night's shocking exchange, I viewed this moment as a pristine launching point to begin offering thanks and praise to my wife.

Within me, an insatiable hunger was now clamoring to give expression to a bottomless gratitude, to acknowledge her and the heavens again and again for the transformative life story that we had shared. And, in truth, I could no more have turned away from the emotional outlets of chanting, prayer, and meditation as abandon a sailboat at sea with no land in any direction.

Whereas the other chants and prayers until now had been specifically intended to invoke blessings that would protect and comfort her on her journey, the purpose of this morning's repetition was simple.

Thank you, Mooch. Thank you for choosing me—for choosing us.
Earl loves you to the moon and back three hundred times.

The Guru Gita is an ancient Indian scripture that takes place in the form of a dialogue between Lord Shiva, the Supreme Guru within, and his beloved Parvati, who is incarnated on Earth. In its opening verses Parvati, with deep devotion, asks him, "By which path can an embodied soul become one with absolute reality?"

Shiva, who in this setting *is* the absolute reality responds, "O

Goddess, you are my very Self. Out of love for you, I will tell you this. No one has ever asked this question before, which is a boon to all mankind."

The next approximately one hundred and eighty *shlokas*, each one containing roughly four verses inside of it, are his reply to her. The chant contains three types of yoga: *bhakti* (devotion), *jnana* (knowledge), and *karma* (action)—all rolled up into an hour of spiritual teachings, abstruse references, and occasionally ecstatic emotions. If that's your thing, and I suppose it is mine, since I have chanted it hundreds of times, it is rife with thought-provoking statements that make worthy companions for years of fruitful contemplation.

In Siddha Yoga, a Guru Gita recitation includes several other chants before and after the text, and now—with the first strains of the introductory melody—my mind and body came into heightened alert while at the same time feeling as soft and supple as rose petals. Moved by what I perceived to be its tender and sacred invitation, tears began to flow amid the distant rumblings of yet another barrier shaking free and crumbling like a sandcastle in the surf.

It soon became obvious to me that this was going to be a Guru Gita unlike any other. Even through its initial sections, like subliminal messenger pigeons, the verses seemed to be carrying unique communications. I was understanding parts of the text as never before. These fresh insights were directly connected to our life together, and began to peel back the edges of an underlying blueprint that was staggering in its scope. Deep, interlacing layers emerged in distinct contrast like strata laid down at another time and place.

Similar to my conversation with Swamiji yesterday, a much larger purpose was gradually allowing itself to be exposed in brief sketches and flashes of intuition. And despite being intricately knit and profound in their impact, each one also struck me as simple and evident as if I was thumbing through the pages of a children's edition of *How Things Work*.

Although unable to grasp the totality of what I was perceiving, its veracity was never in doubt. A powerful current of love and truth gave it the stamp of the real with its unmistakable fingerprint. Rising and falling hypnotically, the underlying message was both rapturous and astounding. This ancient hymn and its sacred sounds were speaking to me of things immutable and everlasting, and though unseen, of a subtle design that had been ever-present and invariably woven throughout all the years of my life.

To say it was moving would be a gross understatement. Gemlike insights were stringing themselves in patterned sequences like glittering diamonds along a gossamer thread, and I was that thread. Serpentlike, the verses uncoiled with arcane elegance and offered me glimpses of a rare, uncharted perspective.

How could I have so shamefully underestimated our bond? I had always believed that I loved Seana with my whole being, and that what we shared as husband and wife was rare and exceptional, and this could never be in doubt. Yet, now I was being informed quite differently. Somehow, it seems that I had grossly undervalued both her and us.

It was as if someone had suddenly folded up an enormous umbrella only to reveal a breathtaking vista that, until now, had been wholly concealed behind it. All at once, around me and exposed in dizzying panoramic relief, lay the historic peaks and canyons of my life like a road map confessing the entire, unbroken journey in one glance. In lines as neat and ordered as rising swells on the sea with rows stacked to the horizon, the view cast my heart to the floor in remorse and left me profoundly humbled.

Somewhere off in the background, another part of me was witnessing this with fascination and wonder. After all, Seana was the love of my life. How was it even possible to have so miscalculated her influence and purpose? And how intriguing that this new information was diminishing neither the memory nor the symmetry of our twelve years together. Quite the contrary, it was exalting us. So that instead of stirring up feelings of guilt for having missed those golden clues to the greater trajectory, I felt blessed beyond belief. I was being permitted to glimpse something extraordinarily beautiful about our relationship that until now had remained veiled.

To receive this knowledge was poignant and magical but to learn of it after the game was finished I found deeply affecting— as if Seana herself were sitting right beside me, blithesome, and giggling her foreknowledge. I began to have the strong suspicion that I had been set up. A ruthless master plan was in play. Ruthless, because it was obvious that the planner had no compunction against using any means necessary to wake me up in this lifetime to a wider view of possibility and purpose.

Nonetheless, as I came around the corners of verse forty-one and forty-two, teetering like a prizefighter in the final round, I walked straight into it, and though sitting cross-legged on the floor, I was laid out.

The verses read, "Salutations to Shri Guru, who appears as the effect [the universe] of which he is the cause. He is the cause as well as the effect.

"All this [the universe] appears in various forms, but there is no difference [in him] from anything. It is merely [an illusion of] cause and effect."

Now, these were verses that I had read and pondered countless times before, yet something about them took me completely by surprise, and within the span of a few seconds an instantaneous series of contemplations was triggered like a ball bouncing down a long flight of stairs.

The cause as well as the effect? No accident? ... She is the cause as well as the effect?

It left me suspended on the outermost edge of something tremendous, but I still could not fathom its implications. It was as if my mind and heart were speaking different languages, so that my ego was left wide open on its blindside, thunderstruck (which pretty much sums up the ego).

Turning my attention to the subsequent verse, I read, "I salute Shri Guru, whose two lotus feet remove the pain of duality and who always protects one from calamities."

Now I was spellbound.

Always protects one from calamities? This was ... not a calamity? She is the cause as well as the effect? If this is not a calamity, then what is it?

In the course of time, I had come to believe that my sadhana, those spiritual practices done for the purpose of freeing myself of conditioned, negative patterns of thinking and feeling, would also offer protection and blessings to my family. In fact, there are many different yogic texts that suggest this very thing—protection offered by the master to a devoted disciple.

And although I am by no means a disciple as I understand that to mean, long before meeting Seana I had fully committed myself to following the path of self-effort and growth as laid out by my Siddha teacher. Over the years, these teachings had proved themselves to me time and again, often providing me with sudden insights as well as what I perceived to be their invisible protection.

And doesn't this verse seem to say that very thing? That my teacher will always protect me and—by supposition and inference from other verses, texts, and teachings—all those I love? So, how could Seana's death not be a calamity?

Abandoning another layer of preconceived ideas, something extraordinary gradually began to show its silhouette, and as the chant progressed, insights continued to unearth themselves like buried treasure. It became more and more apparent that grace had always been present, and that each and every event of my life since receiving shaktipat had been a gift from my teacher. But it was just that I hadn't always had the courage to see it that way.

It was a bit like those connect-the-dots puzzles where you draw a line and slowly the object gets revealed, but a highly-emotional version of it. In this way the greater outline became clearer, then—about halfway through the morning Guru Gita—just like that, in one sudden incandescent flash, I understood.

It's the greater arc! That greater arc of her soul—many lives, not just this one. Only within a larger plan and purpose is this not a terrible calamity!

Immediately, I wondered, *Did we plan this?*

The verses continued to flow on, but I was transfixed by this possibility. Had Seana and I actually planned this whole thing?

The deeper into the chant I moved, the more certain of it I became, until finally it became crystal clear. This entire excruciating event, as well as the possibility of this very moment, had been *designed*. And like some cosmic science experiment, it had a much greater purpose in mind.

Of course, there are lots of holes to be found in this when one looks for them. Still, the incontestable fact was that since her death I was feeling more love, gratitude, and grace than if I had added up all the special and meaningful experiences from my entire life.

This could also be written off as the trauma of losing a loved one, and I *did* make that inference numerous times over the coming year. Yet, what seems clear to me now is that there are very, very few experiences in a lifetime that plainly rise above the rest, and you can question the description and the meaning, but not the event itself.

These rare, prime number episodes may appear to have much in common with other significant and highly emotional moments in our lives, but in the end the immutable truth that they are pointing to can only be recognized by direct experience and *in the present moment*. And more importantly, they can only be certified as transcendently true, or not, by the one perceiving them.

This is because only the perceiver holds the final context and interpretation of his or her life. If it is an authentic communication from a loved one or the one all-pervasive Consciousness, only you can know it. You can even doubt it later, as I did, but that does not prove that it was a limited, transient perception.

I don't remember if there was one specific trigger toward the end of the chant later that morning, or if it was simply the wondrous intersection of an abundance of grace and sheer momentum that untangled the final, bright mystery. If there was any one verse in particular or a series of specific emotions that led to this singular, overwhelming revelation, I am unaware of it. As I said before, I had felt something lurking energetically that morning.

For some of you who are familiar with Kashmir Shaivism, Advaita Vedanta, or any other non-dual philosophy, it may seem obvious and no big deal. But in my state, when it hit me it was mind-blowing, earth-shattering news.

At some point toward the end of the chant, it simply emerged as unmistakably true. *My wife, Seana, is my guru. She and Gurumayi are one!*

In essence and within the context of the Guru Gita, I was

Parvati and Seana was Shiva. And it wasn't just that they had become one now for this particular Guru Gita, or even since Seana had died. The bombshell was in unmasking that they had *always* been one, and I had never recognized it. The Supreme Guru of which the Guru Gita was speaking is that single Divine Power that has become the entire universe and exists within all forms at all times, and it had taken the form of Seana in order to help me grow.

It made me wonder, did Seana know? If one day I had told her that I knew she and my guru were one and the same and in cahoots, would she have agreed? The answer is yes, definitely. Seana had a depth, wisdom, and rascally playfulness that were second only to her self-confidence and unshakable belief that she was here to make a difference, to profoundly impact the world and its creatures for the better.

But did that mean that she was being literal and had attained the same state as my guru, or that she had joined the lineage of Siddhas as guru? No, I don't think so. Although, ultimately how would I know? If we're all One (and it takes one to know one, as the common saying makes quite clear), it can get pretty complicated.

But maybe it wasn't a coincidence that the main topic of the Shaktipat Intensive that I attended on the day Seana died was the five acts of Shiva. Actions One through Three refer to Shiva's *siddhis*, those powers of creation, maintenance, and dissolution of the universe. The fifth and final act, as in *the power to bestow*, is grace. But given the magnitude of the morning's epiphany, of great interest to me was number four on that list, The Act of Concealment. As Seana would say, you don't know what you don't know.

The last strains of the chant drew to a close, leaving me

tear-stained, stunned, and staring at the photos before me in a state of reflective awe.

Wouldn't evidence of this have been present along the way? Shouldn't it have left traces? And while she lived, why wasn't I able to sustain the effort necessary to see beyond appearances?

I regret it with my whole heart. Of all regrets, and I have only a few, I can say that I truly lament missing the opportunity to express my love to her in that way. Because to have done so while she still lived feels to me like it would have been love in action and heaven on earth.

And finally, to have acted on this while she was still alive would simply have been so much fun. It surely would have brought her a great, childlike joy, which Seana deserved unlike anyone I have ever known.

13. Hot Springs

SINCE WE FIRST met, Seana has been a catalyst for transforming so many major, unconscious patterns within me that, as I glance over my fourteen or so journals from our years together, I can only laugh with guilt at the sheer number and intensity of crises that I generated for us in such a short span of time. Apparently, I wanted to learn and grow as much as I possibly could with her. Fortunately, I know that she, too, can laugh about it. Mainly because she did, often directly to my angry, contracted face.

Once the initial surprise had worn off and my old, reactive, emotional upwellings from our first few years together had exposed themselves often enough, Seana developed the infuriating knack of remaining entertained and cheerfully unaffected in the midst of the emotional rollercoaster that was me much of the time. It was maddening her power, and it salvaged the innocence and promise of our marriage more times than I care to count. In one sense, I was like her personal trainer, giving her more than her money's worth in opportunities for personal growth.

WITHIN SIX WEEKS of meeting Seana on my local beach in Hawaii, I was flying to Colorado for a ten-day trial run, and by day seven it had already proven to be much, much more for me than that, and I knew that I was in love with her.

On this particular day, it was late afternoon in the Rocky Mountains, and we were still soaking ourselves in the steamy little pool of a sulphur hot spring.

Out of the blue, she said, "I need to tell you something, but I am afraid it will make you angry. You remember that I am going to meet Joe in a few weeks for my birthday, right? I didn't mention it sooner because I hadn't felt that you shifted yet. I sense a shift now, and it came up that I better tell you."

Unbeknownst to her, this was the most violent of gut punches that I could have ever received. I shuddered and staggered in the steamy pool, held up only by the density of the water around me. Within milliseconds, I had recoiled to the far side of the mineral spring to get away from her.

Seana was totally caught off guard by my reaction and instinctively made a move to cross the gap between us. As soon as she came in my direction, I bolted to the opposite side of the small pool. This repeated itself several times as if we were predator and prey. Feelings of revulsion controlled every muscle in my body, and my face felt contorted into a mix of panic and abhorrence.

For her part, Seana looked utterly stunned. Of course, she couldn't have known what she had summoned from my childhood—primal experiences of betrayal and abandonment.

In unconditional withdrawal and exchanging no other words, I got out of the pool and went into the public bathrooms. Somewhere inside me I understood that I was in the throes of a profound trauma. Past patterns of emotions and fears sprang to life that, like deadly viruses patiently awaiting their moment, had lain dormant for years. Gazing down at my bare feet on the tile, I watched as depression overflowed the rim of who I thought I was in a steady stream of tears and bitter sorrow. Dazed and bewildered, I was fully aware that I had no power to resist or shift out of it, and with this understanding came an unspeakable sadness.

There is an old saying, "When you are afraid, sing to your fear." And so, crestfallen and alone, in full, clear voice beneath the shower, I began to sing to myself. I sang for courage. I sang for hope. I sang for the strength to close the gaping chasm that had opened up and was now flooding the toxic poison of hopelessness into every atom of my being.

Not surprisingly, it was the opening verses from the Guru Gita that arose to comfort and protect me as I sang. The sounds and syllables soared up from me like kites into a clear blue sky in a Morse code message of distress.

Particularly devastating to me was her certainty. The way she had said that she and Joe were *going to go*. Like a trigger on a landmine, it set off an inner sequence of fail-safe alarms from my adolescence, and there was nothing more deeply hardwired into my being than fear of betrayal. It was to be avoided at any and all costs. From that moment forward, I heard nothing else she said, and my mind was no longer my own.

The car ride together down the mountain was absolute torture. Seana drove, and she wanted answers. The sun had just set, and the deep canyon, trees, and sky were all flushed and bloodshot in reddish-pinks, violet, and an orange glow. I tried my best not to leap out of the car and run full speed on foot back to the house for my luggage. This reactive pattern of terror and abandonment was primitive, and its seeds and origin stories had been sown very deep and at a tender age.

"You said, 'I love you,' and that I am your ideal man, your ideal lover. Your words and actions conveyed a deep intimacy between us, and that I was the one you were looking for."

"No, they did not. That was not until today when we were discussing last night, and then your breakthrough earlier about not being able to help your mother."

"Our morals are different regarding how to act in this situation, Seana."

"I don't think it has anything to do with my morals at all. It has more to do with your story and judgment around what you think we agreed to coming into this Colorado visit. We never promised we would be exclusive. We said we would see other people when we were apart and see how it goes once you came. For your visit we were looking at the *possibility* of a committed relationship. Just the *possibility*."

Though on the outside the scene in the car was relatively calm and our voices were not raised, it felt as if I was fighting for my life. Kindled somewhere within was fiery outrage along with a bleak, core numbness. It felt highly explosive and flammable—and eerily familiar.

"Then, I made assumptions that were wrong. I assumed that in agreeing to the possibility of a committed relationship we were holding ourselves free and completely open for this immense possibility. You never mentioned this date with Joe, a special weekend over your birthday and a ten-year reunion. I was sure that I was by far and away your first choice. I was wrong."

There was a long, silent pause.

Arising inside me now was a powerful desire to quickly move on and abandon any hope of a future together. Perhaps this was what seemed so familiar. This wish felt like an old friend and guardian protector, intimately knowledgeable of both past and present. With it, I prepared to barricade myself from the immense sadness that was now multiplying at an exponential rate.

In the midst of the strongest of these emotions, she asked, "Can you wait for me, Barron?"

"Did you arrange those plans with him when we were emailing one another from Hawaii?"

"No, I think we decided that in May before I came to Hawaii."

Another pause ensued.

"You told me before I came that when you kissed Joe after Hawaii you told him that you would not be in any contact with him from then until after my visit. The way you shared this convinced me that I was your first choice. You even said that while you were kissing him you were distracted while doing it. At the time, it felt like you were trying to ease my doubts."

"You were a *possibility* of being my first choice. That was all."

Once again that word stung, and I replied, "How could you set up this visit as a *possibility* of a committed relationship while you have someone else waiting in the wings, another possible man to fill the same role?"

"Because I can. There is no conflict there for me."

"Wow! I had no idea that you were like this. I could never do that to someone in that situation."

There was an even longer silence. I watched the road and river swiftly passing away before and beside us, an undulating ribbon of white, blue, and silver that stayed parallel to the highway even as it threaded its way down the canyon. It was so beautiful just outside the car, no hint of conflict between trees and cliffs, sunlight and shadow. Nature seemed to have an enduring ability to effortlessly coexist.

From past experience, I recognized this as the moment I turn to her and write it all off with one last gesture of defiance and then, as fast as my credit card would allow, escape back to Hawaii.

Yet, this all seemed so familiar—the disappointing end with the disillusioning woman. And of course, it called for a final good-bye; that signature move that both mocks with contempt and flips the finger in fierce independence. From just beyond the outer boundary of my personal story, I could not see so much as feel the falseness hidden within the intensity of the melodrama. It was of my own creation.

Wasn't I just that angry child still blaming the outside world for his fears? Had I forgotten my strange fascination with watching intimate relationships fall apart? Once more, the grand play that had at first blossomed with promise was now contracting in fear. Next would come complete withdrawal with an acute and resigned melancholy. For hadn't sadness been woven into the very fabric of my childhood? Not once, but twice, my mother rising so high and then plummeting darkly across and downward through two marriages. The first through selfishness, boredom and betrayal—and the second in violence and abuse.

Though I did not make the conscious connection in the moment—my body, mind, and emotions recognized these felt-patterns as old friends. Disloyalty, rejection, hopelessness, despair, and escape stood by in an unbroken chain, passed along like batons in a relay race or a family inheritance.

And yet, Seana was different, and I knew it in my core. No matter what evidence I may have gathered to the contrary, she seemed to exude a nobility and goodness. There was the presence of an almost effortless integrity in her words which I found unde-niable in spite of my efforts to prove her guilt.

It had been quiet in the car for quite some time. The visual beauty of the drive down the mountain pass added a poignance and counterweight to what now felt like it had been the climax not only of our conversation but of our brief relationship.

Looking out the window, I suspected that I had very little time left. I could feel myself teetering precariously on the edge. Straddling the boundary between my past, present, and future, I caught a flash and an intuition. I sensed that I desperately wanted more than I ever had before and that I was also ready for it, or at least to try for it.

But even though we were sitting right beside one another, I was so very far from where she was and from where I wanted to be. It would take something extraordinary to climb out of this deep hole, an act of singular courage and vulnerability, and I had no idea where to begin. And then, would she even want me after having seen how dramatic and fragile I could be?

Down the canyon, dusk was slowly advancing across the sky in darker violets and reds. The landscape was rushing by, and it neither slowed down nor stopped. With that, I understood that both Seana and the heaviness I felt were windows of opportunity that would not last. Sadness was becoming desperation. I needed to make a definitive choice.

Just beneath the surface of this despair, I could still make out the shape of hope standing by and shining like a tiny beacon of light, awaiting even the narrowest of openings. If I could only just somehow begin to put down this staggering weight that had reduced me to barely a wisp of a ghost and stripped me of all recognizable qualities, there might still be a chance.

All at once, I understood once and for all that I did not want to give up, and that I longed to try, regardless of the cost. I suddenly was willing to risk everything, and with that astonishing impulse, the smothering grip around my heart softened just enough for me to reach out for help.

Turning to look at her for the first time in what seemed like an eternity, I asked, "What do you do when you want to focus on the love, but you're feeling hurt?"

With no hesitation, Seana answered, "You sense a smile in your heart area for the situation."

"Like the quote that says there is something more important than the fear?"

"Yes."

And just like that, the journey to Seana and to seeing myself whole again, began.

THE FOLLOWING MORNING, I am lying in her bed feeling slightly lighter. But before I have even fully awakened, I hear a very clear message in my head. As I rise from the bed, I take it to heart and into my morning meditation.

You must shift the focus away from anger and hurt. Make the effort to re-open the relationship in whatever form it takes.

In spite of my best efforts, however, as we begin the morning drive up to Gold Lake a few hours later for a couple's massage that was scheduled weeks ago, I find myself once again trapped high above us on the same frozen trails. Withheld and altogether aware that Seana may not be interested in sticking around for this act much longer, the weight pulls at me like gravity.

Since last night, I have been working ceaselessly on this with one-pointed intention, meditating, journaling, and praying with all my heart. Apparently, I still have a long way to go. In a moment of clarity, I understand that it is getting late, and I may not make it to the gate in time.

On the drive back up the mountain, there is almost no conversation. Seana knows I am working hard to get free, but seems to have detached herself from the end result. This makes me focus even more intently.

All morning long I have felt such heaviness and a subtle depression blocking my every effort to break out. A current of darkness and lethargy flows intermittently through my body and thoughts, holding me captive with little progress to show for so many hours of clear intention and effort. It seems like an unceasing and almost impossible struggle to rise out of this paralysis, like a hot air balloon that has been staked tightly to the ground. The deep patterns just seem to have no end to their cycles, and I am neither freer nor lighter than before.

For much of the drive, I have my headphones in and listen to excerpts of talks from various teachers, silently repeat the mantra, and watch my inner state in a game of hide-and-seek. Seesawing in exaggerated leaps between hopeful and hopeless, I am so afraid that I may already know the outcome. In truth, I have been working on this one for many years, and I have seen how it turns out. Thus, I teeter from trusting to fearful and back again like a cobra striking at its own reflection in the water.

Nevertheless, having traveled this path for so long, I am aware of the importance in challenging times to just keep going. So, though I am desperate, I remain in steady movement. And consequently, just like that, by staying in constant, intentional motion, I stumble upon the seed of the suffering. From this one blue atom, all of my fears have grown outward like intricately laced branches in a genealogically rooted tree. Since even before I can remember having a memory, these networks have subtly influenced every choice I have ever made.

The paralyzing fear of *what if*. *What if* I am unable to …? *What if* I do not succeed? *What if* the worst possible outcome happens? And this mantra of defeat and hopelessness will simply not erase.

As a young boy, I lived through years of family trauma at home. That little boy witnessed the chaos and aftermath so many times that he is already convinced he knows the outcome. Thus, every time anything threatens to turn out badly, unconsciously he hears repeating in his head, *This is how it really is. And this is how it really is. And this is how it always will be.*

It's a sound loop, a vibration and mantra so deeply hardwired that one could legitimately wonder, *Who would I be without this fear?* and actually not know the answer. But that is the right question.

So, how well I know that my rescue cannot come from Seana nor anyone else for that matter. Yet, how badly I need the help. This is why I am listening to my teachers, replacing the old mantras and laying down new soundtracks. Perhaps it is the reason I started meditation, yoga, and self-study so long ago as if in training for these moments. I have always known they would come. Indeed, one of my closest childhood friends who I grew up surfing with, upon hearing of Seana's sudden death told my other dear surfing-buddy, "It's a good thing he has been meditating and doing that spiritual stuff for so long."

As if I need one last metaphor for what life is like inside a deeply embedded negative pattern, morning fog in smoky, white wisps descends over the hills for the last few miles of the long drive reducing the visibility to only a few yards. We will just make it to the massage in time.

Just as we're entering the parking lot of the mountain resort, the mist has begun lifting. Quite suddenly, and without warning of any kind, something simply falls into place like the final piece in an invisible puzzle.

I will be fine without Seana. I can let her go. I can wish her well.

With these thoughts, it's as if I have been awakened from a

profound nightmare. Out of the blue, whether or not Seana and I will be together matters little. For at least these first few moments, I feel like I am swiftly rising up, soaring high above the car and a terrible, suffocating dream. Liberated of the immense weight of *being me*, I fly free, out and above my physical body like a leaf that has caught a sudden gust of wind. No burden, and no need to try and control her, remain. After so many hours of struggle and intense judgment, it feels miraculous in every sense of the word.

The fog has now burned off almost completely and, as if conjured by fairies, all around us has sprung up a wildly beautiful landscape of yellow, green, and lavender wildflowers beneath a deep-blue sky. Feathery, white clouds meander slowly across its immense cerulean canvas, dotting it sporadically with spots of fluff like a celestial Dalmatian dog.

Feeling incredibly light, optimistic, and fearless too, I turn to Seana for the first time in hours and smile genuinely at her. It has been a very rough ride, and I am honestly relieved to at last be able to send her a glance of kindness and empathy. This must have been quite an ordeal for her, too, because she looks back at me, her eyes wide in surprise and gratitude. In truth, the shift within me is in such sharp contrast to the previous hours that I am almost ecstatic. Exiting the car, I continue saying silent prayers for this expansive feeling to please, please stay.

14. Gold Lake

GOLD LAKE MOUNTAIN Spa and Resort is one hundred acres of rustic elegance. Abutting the resort, the prairie and shoreline are painted in vibrant, native flowers with unobstructed views of snow-white, fourteen-thousand-foot peaks. Hiking trails are sprinkled throughout with extraordinary sculptures that are beautiful not just because they add charm and loveliness via large, outdoor sculpture art, but also in how they're intentionally designed to enhance one's experience of the natural environment.

At the resort office, I can tell my expanded state is still with me because I am light and giddy as we meet our masseuses, Stephanie and Monica. A brief walk to the cabin takes us outdoors along a lovely, wooded trail, and I am like a small child delighting in everything around me.

Gratitude for this profound turnaround reverberates palpably throughout my limbs and into the way I see and feel everything we pass by—the amber pine tree bristles with their delicious, pungent aroma; the angle of sunshine shooting arrows of golden light between the branches and down onto the rust-brown soil of the earth; the crunch-crunch of small stones and pebbles beneath our shoes. These sights and sounds feel rich and cathartic, communicating the cheerful, celebratory aura of a hard-won freedom.

Inside the room, our massage tables are just a few feet apart, and climbing up under the white sheet and onto the pad, I can't help but notice a distinct stillness. Soft music, fragrant aromas, and candlelight soothe every part of me, relaying the pleasant sensations of surrender within a protected haven. Instinctively, and even before lying down, I take complete refuge in this cabin room, and my frayed nerves and breathing release in agreement and relief.

My masseuse Stephanie is young, strong, and quite beautiful. As she begins to massage me, I think to myself, *Thank you, Gurumayi, for your protection throughout this.* Then I begin to imagine that she is present, that she is the one massaging me.

In my mind, I repeat, *Stephanie's hands are Gurumayi's hands. Let her hands be Gurumayi's hands. Please, Gurumayi, be here with me now. Let your hands be her hands. Thank you, Gurumayi. Thank you, Gurumayi. Thank you with all my heart.*

Within seconds of these thoughts, there is a palpable shift along the skin of my body wherever Stephanie's hands press against me. It is unmistakable. Tangible and electric, wherever she is touching me becomes absolutely blissful. This makes me ecstatic. Filling with a strange sort of rapture unlike anything I have ever known, the last walls of my defenses and fear simply vanish. I have no need for them now, and as if released by some mysterious, unlooked-for boon, the feeling of reprieve is immense.

Here in my body and magnifying along my skin, uncharted physical sensations send tingling electricity up and down my back. Behind my eyes, light from a sudden unearthly luster intensifies until, quite abruptly, I feel around me the warmth of a cave. It is glittering with light. An overwhelming sense of protection and gratitude pervades every particle of my awareness, and I hear my own voice in my mind saying, *I have been holding off the fear for so long now, and with your help I am letting it go, forever.*

The tears that had been slipping down both sides of my face in split, parallel streams now begin to unload. It's as if a slight mist gave way to a sudden rain that disgorges its entire payload onto bone-dry land. In thundercracks and torrential cloudbursts, I am soaked, entranced, and far beyond the reach of caring what anyone who is looking upon this scene may be thinking. Surrendering myself completely to the bliss of it, I can sense Gurumayi's absolute protection and guiding love all around me and throughout the cabin. It's as if she is holding me tenderly in her arms, and I weep openly and without reserve.

If you could imagine being a small child again and constrained to hold out in terror above an abyss of what feels like certain annihilation, manage to claw your way back from its edge, and then quite unexpectedly and unconditionally be rescued from it, you will have a sense of how I feel on that table.

Very soon, my attention becomes drawn to a second intense gathering of scintillating light just inside my closed eyelids. The mass of light focuses itself, tightening into one single point, and then pulses outward forming into the small circle of a shimmering halo. And there, within that ring of light, slowly appears the face of my teacher, Gurumayi.

Utterly in awe, I watch as it floats before me. She is completely inward-looking and content within her own pure state, yet also gazing at me. Then the edges of her face slowly begin to vibrate and blur reorganizing itself into the compassionate face of her own guru, Baba Muktananda. I am completely filled with wonder. In amazement, I think to myself, *This is really happening. This is real!*

Floating before me, Baba is gazing at me with a depth of love and compassion that is unlike anything I have ever seen. No one has ever looked at me in this way before, and I accept it as a profound gift, humbled and stunned. Eventually, the edges of his face slowly blur until they merge back into Gurumayi's. Completely suspended in amazement, I watch as the sequence continues with each of their faces appearing, disappearing, and merging into one another in a way that seems to also convey equality and oneness.

At some point in the cycle, the next face to appear is Seana's. Kind and pure, luminous like the moon, it is surrounded by the exact same lustrous light. But it feels so immediately out of place that I have the thought, *No! That's not right. What is her face doing here among my gurus?* I am so caught off guard that I almost say it out loud.

But none of my reaction has any effect on Seana's face or expression whatsoever. Gradually her glowing, benevolent face dissolves and merges back into Gurumayi's face. This loop continues for another round or two, and the messages I am receiving are clear: *There is no need to fear or doubt any of this. The Siddhas' love and promise have never been stronger. They will never abandon you.*

Awestruck and humbled, I say silently, *I love you, Baba. I love you, Gurumayi—with all of my being. You are true and I am never out of your divine and loving glance. All of my deepest prayers to you from my sadhana are in fruition.*

Before long, the visions begin to gently recede. Their glowing faces spark and fizzle, gradually dissolving into particles of soft, gold light and satiny silvers. The remaining auroras now coalesce tightly together once again into a focal point on the inside of my eyelids.

Still pulsing within me, vivid and sublime, is a feeling of supreme protection and profound gratitude like a heavenly perfume that permeates everything. It feels as if mountains of accumulated dust and dirt from many lifetimes of negative thoughts and fears are being washed away.

Several times I have to ask Stephanie for tissues to blow my dripping nose and wipe my shiny, wet face. That there are others in the room is of no concern to me at all. Perhaps they're wondering what is going on. But if they're aware of me at all, it seems obvious that they understand this to be a rare and uplifting experience, and no one interrupts or speaks.

After a while, very sweetly and compassionately, Stephanie invites me to turn over onto my stomach. In her voice, I hear wonderment. At this natural pause in the massage, I feel like I ought to offer some brief word of explanation. But before I am able to find my voice, the motion of turning myself over on the table triggers the release of fresh, new waves that roll through me like a heavy squall in a cyclone. Once again, I am weeping uncontrollably, dragged out to sea by the stronger pull of the current.

A brief interval between swells permits me to catch my breath before the next one arrives. In between two of its most blissful waves and with my eyes still closed, the incomparable gift that this is suddenly crystallizes. It pierces me so profoundly that I say aloud to the room, "The gratitude is so huge!"

And with that, the immensity of the discovery becomes almost bewildering. I hear myself saying in astonishment, "I had no idea that I am so loved!"

Another wave of ecstasy sweeps me up high above its glorious crest and then tenderly redeposits me again at the trough. In the ensuing interval, a genuine childlike wonder turns to amazement, and in one of the most poignant moments of my life, it all coalesces. There are no more words left to describe what is happening.

"How did I forget this?"

Addressed to no one in particular, this question is among the truest I will ever ask. From completely absent to unmistakably present, the sheer generosity of this experience is so striking that it feels like I have woken up from total amnesia. A profound sense of reverence and innocence pervades my body and vision such that I cannot remember ever having experienced anything like it even as a young boy.

In the serene wake of the passing storm, my entire body is humming and crackling with delicious vibrations. Everything around me is softly sparkling, and I'm unsure if my eyes are open or closed. But wherever I am, a feeling of deep contentment and fulfillment buzzes through my being. Looking outward, I behold golden sparks glistening in the walls, the corners of the room, the cotton sheet that covers my legs, the glow of the lamp and candle—anywhere that my glance roams.

Have you ever felt something like this? Perhaps it came as a sheen of blessedness that for a moment blanketed everything around you like snowfall. Or it's possible you glimpsed it as you were standing alone in your kitchen just after your children, happy and excited, had all left for school or for a sleepover.

Maybe a tiny sliver of a crescent moon visited you as you were sitting in your car one night (for that is more than enough for a lifetime) after a lengthy, arduous task had been successfully completed. Quietly seated, you took in one long, spontaneous inhalation, and as you exhaled with a protracted sigh, totally letting go, no thought came in to replace it.

Wherefore, in that ensuing stillness, a deep and dreamlike peacefulness shone forth, scattering scintillating light through every particle across the length and breadth of the street in all directions. Mesmerized, you watched it pass into the other automobiles with their drivers all at rest, and sat there in wide-eyed wonder just as you have seen your own children do so many times since their births.

The massage is coming to an end, and just before exiting the room the other masseuse, Monica, turns to Seana and me. With a look of deep respect, she says, "I feel honored to have been in the room to share that with you."

Alone at last, Seana and I look at each other for the first time since entering the cabin. Her glance says so much, but she declares it in words anyway, and so, claims me.

"I am deeply, passionately, vulnerably, and tenderly in love with you—with the beauty that you are."

PERHAPS AT THE time, I chose to rest there with my questioning because I felt that this unique experience was perfect just as it was and more than enough. But in any case, I don't delve deeper into the mystery of this gift and its uncommon symbolism.

So, I miss it—the fullness of what has actually been given. Grateful to have been rescued, astonished to have started a relationship with a radiant goddess, I am like a thief running out of a jewelry store, arms filled with cash while the diamonds remain behind in the display counter coruscating their unimaginable wealth.

Doubtless, a key reason why Seana's face appeared among my teachers was for me to understand, once and for all, that we had their blessings as a couple. And afterwards, to the extent that my samskara would allow, I did stop running away from her. Nonetheless, I had been lifted into a different world in that room, a once-in-a-lifetime supernatural experience of grace and transcendent love and gratitude, and yet all I end up taking away from it is that I am deeply blessed and loved, and that Seana and I are supposed to be together.

Had I eyes to see and a humble heart, that rare event could have also revealed its treasure trove and the melodic counterpoint to one of the underlying purposes of my life. But, in spite of my teachers going to all this trouble, that is something I won't unravel for another twelve years, when her sudden and final disappearance will occupy my full and undivided attention.

Seana and my guru are one and the same. They abide in light together and come from the same Source—her face alongside their faces, pulsing and throbbing divine gifts and mysteries out into the universe.

LIKE A SWOLLEN river rising up the banks and its inevitable descent, by mid-afternoon the shocking revelations of the morning Guru Gita have begun to subside. I reread what I posted earlier in the morning and go online to see what people are saying about it. In addition to the many condolences, I notice that I am repeatedly drawn to rereading what I wrote. It's like a craving. Each time I read the words, I feel struck by what I perceive to be their poignant beauty.

Yet, I also sense that something else is lurking in this experience. There's something important happening. After reading the post again, I scan my awareness. It's as if a large pocket has opened up inside, leaving me hollower than before. The deep connection with my heart that has been my constant companion since I heard the officer say, "She is deceased," is suddenly missing.

It's such an immediate, obvious shift in how I feel, like a scene in three dimensions that suddenly switches to two, that all at once everything feels flat and shallow.

What in the world happened?

I look at the words that I have posted, again. Rereading them gives me pleasure, but I am suspicious now. In my head, I remember something that my teacher once said. Two things will lead you directly to your downfall—the sense of self-importance and the craving for the good opinion of others. Both seem to be at work here.

In my mind, I ask Swamiji to protect me from this thing that is sneaking into the once-in-a-lifetime opportunity of grieving and loving beyond measure. It divides and separates, masquerading as me. Keenly aware of the danger, I cannot allow it.

Out of the blue, I hear in my head, *Tell yourself that if you do either of those two things that Baba warned about, then Seana loses the gifts and blessings from your words.*

At that, my mind goes completely silent. Message received.

I make a firm resolution to keep a vigilant watch for any signs of self-importance or the craving for good opinions creeping into my thoughts, words, and actions. It's not complicated. It just requires willpower, and far too much is at stake for me not to do it.

So, I start speaking aloud to Seana as if she is standing right next to me.

"Amore, when I lose presence through thought and imagined conversations with others, I lose connection to you. No matter how uplifted they may appear to be. I must watch it!"

With this declaration, throughout the day, as thoughts come in to land I begin to study them much more closely. Those conversations that I hear in my head are taking up a lot of energy and time, but they're neither necessary nor beneficial. Performing for an imaginary audience, they pull me out and away so that I'm no longer in my heart moment-to-moment. They make me feel very good, but the cost is far too great. I lose everything I love.

Later that afternoon, I try it out again. In the middle of a beauty of an imaginary conversation to a group of friends, I catch myself. Pausing, I ask Seana if she has heard or felt any of these words from the internal discussion? There is complete silence in my head—a definite *no*.

Immediately, I try shifting my awareness to being present here and now, empty of thoughts and especially free of any thought-conversations with others. In that space, a clear channel to my heart tangibly opens up like a corridor. Or, perhaps more accurately, I become the inner corridor, and out of nowhere, once again *I am* great love and loss. Only seconds before, there was nothing but a very small version of me standing before the open window of the cottage looking upon the blue Salish Sea. Now, everything feels real, connected and meaningful—free from any opinion or the need to label it.

Intrigued, I start experimenting with this phenomenon. Making my espresso, the first sip is offered to Seana. I envision her sitting on the stool next to me and savoring its bittersweet taste, taking pleasure in the act through my five senses.

Inspired by the apparent success, for the gates have remained open, I say aloud, "Okay, so my new goal is to share the *last* sip of espresso with you too."

As soon as I say this, I burst out laughing and feel with near absolute certainty that Seana is giggling too at the steep mountain that this particular challenge will be for me. Fast forward to one minute later, the last sip is gone and I forgot to share it with her. More laughter. This is a very good development.

Out loud I say to the room, "There are still a few last drops. I am delighting in your love of the smell of fresh espresso and your deep satisfaction in my delight as I sip it. I love you so much, Amore."

Interestingly, as I begin to check in more often, conversations out loud to her do not have the same effect of separating me from my heart. Quite the opposite—I feel deeply connected. I have no idea why this is so, but I am very glad for it.

Days Five & Six

15. Sense-Making

A LONG WITH ALL of this sense-making, there are things to do. So, the next morning I research mortuaries in Colorado that offer cremation services while also booking a flight to Colorado. I begin to pack and likewise accept the invitation of a dear friend in Hawaii to come and continue my healing in her empty apartment on the island of Oahu.

On my phone, I see a message from the Colorado Police Victims Advocate Department. It's a service provided by the state when an automobile accident results in death. Hearing his voicemail is yet another side of this hourly coin toss delivering untold gifts with ruthless brutality. It acts as an abrupt, rocklike reminder that I am a fluttering leaf amid forces far beyond my capacity to comprehend.

Packing for Colorado and Hawaii happens in impulsive bursts of movement like heating popcorn but without the final satisfaction. I am indeed the creature of habit that Seana loved to laugh about and tease. However, with the exception of referencing my past lists for the different locations I will visit, my packing routine today is neither commonplace nor predictable, and soon every surface in the cottage is draped with clothing.

It is a fascinating and surreal play, this hopping back and forth from one reality to another, and a tangible expression of life flowing onward whether I wish it to or not. Like the dappled sunlight on our rambling forest path, this attention to duties sweetly draws me in such that I also find myself noticing the exquisite tenderness that imbues the cottage this afternoon.

Still, every now and then, in the pauses, I find myself wishing that everything would just stop and mourn with me awhile.

16. The Mortuary

DIRECT FROM THE airport, it was well after midnight when I first walked into the room that Seana last occupied in Colorado. I remember pausing to look down at the threshold right before entering. Lined up in neat rows just inside the door were several pairs of her shoes. Farther inside, everything had been left carefully arranged for the flight home that she would not catch. In a snapshot literally frozen in time, clues to her final moments were everywhere. It was like walking into a crime scene.

When you share nearly every minute of twelve years with someone, you come to know all their nuances. Staring into the shadows of the bedroom before me, it appeared as if my beloved had just gone upstairs for a few minutes and could be expected to walk right back in at any moment, apologize for the temporary mess, and then finish her packing. Like a history lesson's primary source photograph, it offered a window into a lost moment in time that was hard to acknowledge.

Perhaps most unsettling of all was how she had laid everything out so intentionally. Clothing, jewelry, supplements, journals, gifts, books she was reading, articles she was studying and highlighting, all spread before me. Fanning outward like a Ferris wheel from her open suitcase in the center of the small room and covering nearly every surface were the property and last signs of a beautiful life.

Instantly, I understood how completely unprepared for this moment I was. Overpowered by emotions too complex and numerous to give names, I knelt down, touched the floor and my heart, and then stepped inside. There on the bed amid stacks of her folded clothing I found an open space, curled up like a sow bug, and wept.

I'M ON THE phone with the mortuary, and the owner keeps trying to talk me out of seeing Seana's body before her cremation.

"This is isn't the way you will want to remember her. The accident caused injuries that I won't be able to hide with makeup or anything else, really."

"I understand. Just do what you can, please. I'll see you this afternoon."

In spite of this phone conversation, I am not at all sure that I want to see Seana's body. I don't know if I'll actually show up later at the funeral parlor doors.

What am I thinking? What good could possibly come from it? What's the point? Why don't I just let go of this?

Colorado. Where we lived most of our married life together is also the place where it ends. Every familiar sight is layered like a soft-focus filter in a movie, each with an alternate reality where things appear to look the same but feel completely different.

Though I am in a car, it's as if I am flying high overhead and seeing each neighborhood fresh and new but simultaneously outdated and worn. Friendly highways and vistas are now colored differently than I remember them, especially Highway 66. I feel detached and like I am done here, as if this place that ended Seana has ended for me too.

Interestingly, there is no bitterness. While every emotion one might expect has passed through me, anger was and is still not one of them. It's the combined grace of Seana and sadhana, again. The greater arc has swept me up and is now holding me detached in the air high above this wide, flat land like I'm a puffy white cloud drifting up and away over its miles-high, snow-capped mountain border. There is nothing here for me anymore, and I feel neither remorse nor a pining for the good old days.

There is, however, today. Though I may be wandering somewhat aimlessly through Longmont traffic, the thought of Seana's body and its cremation is drawing me in tighter and tighter concentric circles. Her body pulls at me uncomfortably, and yes, I know it is not her, and I do think I understand that if I go to the viewing of her body, I will only see an empty shell. *But what will be my experience?* That's the unknown. That's the possibility that does not feel like it should be run from. I have just this one shot at choosing well. No do-overs.

Our dear friends here in Loveland and Denver are equally uncertain about what to do. Seana's disappearance has unbalanced them, too, and I sense their fragility and lack of clarity. I will be forever grateful for their loving, open arms, and I rest protected at least in part by their love for Seana, and for me, too. But in some ways, I feel infinitely clearer and more grounded in my heart than a few of them appear to be.

One brave soul offers to give me a ride to the mortuary this afternoon. I ask her if she wants to see Seana's body, but she doesn't think so. At the last minute, two more close friends of ours offer to come along for support. Neither of them wishes to see the body either, and I am still unclear whether or not I will. I just can't see the point.

As we pull into the mortuary parking lot, it suddenly comes

clear. That I don't see the point is not the point. It's the looking that matters. This is precisely why I need to be alone with her body. To stay open to whatever it is that might be waiting in that room. I really need to ignore my mind more often.

The small mortuary is located in a tiny strip mall, and does indeed have a smell. It's not like I can detect dead bodies or anything, but there is a damp, closed-in scent in the one-room office. There's also an eerie, mostly black and brown painting of the owner on the wall, so that he is both standing before us speaking and within the portrait behind him frozen in time like an observant dead character in a Harry Potter book.

Next door is the parlor viewing room. Both the office and the funeral parlor beside it have one set of windows for the entire wall facing out upon the adjacent parking lot. I leave my three friends and get led inside the viewing room by the owner.

Left alone, I see that the parlor is already set up for the next public service with white folding chairs lining both sides of the aisle. Impenetrable curtains block the bright Colorado sun, and I have an hour if I want that long.

Directly across from me in the room lies Seana's body. It's on a table against the far wall and mostly concealed by a white sheet, but I can see her head protruding from the covering.

Amore mio! What has happened to you, my beloved?

It is an abrupt reaction like the sudden cracking of a mirror, and the view from where I stand is terrible and timeless. What kind of ending is this for that beautiful soul? It seems utterly incongruous with the way she lived every minute of her life.

But following immediately on its heels comes a pronounced feeling of boundless love. It rushes through me with such otherworldly tenderness that all at once I know this is right. I can feel it everywhere in my body, my heart, and vibrating in the room too.

And with this precipitous understanding comes an acceptance and a clarity that I am supposed to be here. It's sacred. My breath instinctively deepens, and a wave of relaxation and anticipation electrifies me.

This solitary act of entering a chamber with death could have been many things today, but somehow, I forgot sacred. How is it that I forgot this as a possibility? Yet, I almost didn't come. But that, too, makes perfect sense now. Unable to imagine anything but the fear, how could I possibly imagine what might lie beyond it?

Seana's disappearance has changed all that. Standing here, I see and feel that there is actually nothing but the sacred all around me. Perhaps there never has been.

Within this little room where life and death are permitted to meet, eternity prevails. The familiar sweetness of who Seana and I are for one another permeates my senses, softening shoulders, jaw, cheeks, and my gaze. This is exactly where I need to be because *it still is* who we are for each other. I can't believe how close I came to not coming here. Good god, I almost missed this honoring of her form.

Just before moving forward, my hand instinctively touches my heart, and then I walk slowly down the aisle toward her. In my backpack are items for offering blessings, and I set the bag down before taking the final few steps to her body. Only her neck, face, and blonde hair can be seen. Her left eye is closed, and her right eye and part of her forehead are covered with an improvised head-band. That must be what the owner didn't want me to see.

But instead of aversion, there is only immense gratitude rising up inside. What a gift to have known her! What blessings too numerous to count to have spent even a few hours by her side, let alone twelve years. How fortunate I was.

I reach out and discover through the sheet that her arm is cold and stiff. Though I should have anticipated this, it immediately jolts me back to the competing narratives. Her face doesn't quite look like the Seana I know and love. It's not that it is disfigured, but nevertheless the expression and countenance aren't fully hers—maybe because it is motionless and Seana was always in animated motion, her radiant smile and laughter spreading to all around like a forest fire or a kaleidoscope of butterflies migrating home, all color and movement.

This reminds me that in the days immediately following her death, Colorado's entire Front Range was inundated by an early and unusually large migration of Painted Ladies. "Clouds of butterflies" were reported across three states.

Though her face shows some of the wear and tear of her final hour, her golden hair is soft to the touch. It feels just like I remember it. Gently, and with the tips of my fingers, I stroke it along the curve of her head and around the ear, marveling at how it alone has kept its delicate, smooth texture.

Doing this strains the boundaries of the moment, and an emptiness arises where only seconds before there was bliss. Standing over her body and running my fingers through the waves of hair that frame her pale face brings to mind the trauma that she suffered at the end. So far, I have been able to avoid this element of the story, but no longer.

Oh Amore, I am so sorry I was not able to be there for your suffering.

This realization strikes a blow so acute that for a moment my lungs shut down and no breath will come. Until now, I have not permitted any thoughts regarding the violence of her end.

On my phone are photos that I have ready just in case I needed a reminder of her vibrant beauty, her innate and unforgettable spirit. Pulling up my favorite one, I place the small screen next to her head on the table so that it is obvious that she is absent in the one and dynamically present in the other. Ah, yes! *That* is my beloved, not this empty husk. The two narratives merge and both are given permission to exist simultaneously, just as they do on the table before me. One is temporarily true while the other was, is, and continues to be.

But, oh, what a spectacular, hypnotizing guise this was for her to take, and what beauty and purity went along for the ride. This is what I want to honor now—the temporary form that she moved through and as. This physical body gave her everything it had to give, right up to the end like a humble, faithful devotee. If only I could have served her as perfectly as this body of hers.

The table upon which she lies now becomes an altar. Fresh flowers are arranged and photos of revered saints line the back of it. Although those great beings have also left their physical forms, once the photographs are all in a row, it's easy to envision each one briefly coming present in the room, almost like on a video-call where people's photos gradually get replaced online by their live-action selves.

Less than an hour before this, another dear friend living in the upstate New York ashram sent me a recording of special Sanskrit mantras that she and a few others had gathered to sing just for this occasion, though they had never known Seana. More acts of kindness to stir my heart and invoke an auspicious ending to an exceptional life.

The syllables and their unique melodic lines spill softly into the silence of the room, slowly filling it with an unmistakable aura. I light a small votive candle and watch mesmerized as its warm glow spreads over the sheet and across her face.

Lifting the candle up in both hands, I bow my head to it and to her and begin waving the tiny flame. Slowly, the rings of golden light circle clockwise around her entire body, toe to head, and around the line of photos, too. The sound of the mantras and the flickering flame bring to my awareness the felt-presence of all these beings. In my mind, Seana is with them now, and an indescribable serenity fills the chamber. Every time the flame passes in front of their eyes, a primordial ritual as old as life itself swirls through me with an almost aching current of electricity.

All at once—gratitude, wild and deep as a river, bursts forth, overflowing its banks. Though it is happening within me, it also fills the room around me. Somewhere deep within, a long-hidden aquifer has been pierced, and tears of love roll down my cheeks, onto my sleeves, the white sheet, and the table and floor below.

Nectar is bubbling up and I am lost, completely disappearing into the undulating flame and the ecstasy of what she and I are when we come together. Though no confirmation of this truth is needed, for it is simple and obvious, its evidence glistens in whatever my eyes rest upon.

I have forgotten to breathe, and a huge inhalation brings everything back at once, shifting the focus of my perception. Now the eyes of the saints have come alive, and their compassion and depth are astonishing and real.

How extraordinary!

A tiny diamond in the center of each pair of eyes shimmers in micromovements, and they make their presence known. This causes me to cry out softly in surprise.

In my mind, I bow to each one with my whole heart for being present to honor Seana. It feels as if they're also acknowledging us—the mysterious goodness that was drawn out even when all seemed lost, like when I almost left her, how many times?

I am so sorry for that, too, Amore mio. That was one of my biggest lessons and you carried me through far too many times, often on your back.

When the mantras finish playing, the small candle is placed on one of the white chairs next to me in the front row. I feel amazing. This is not how I expected this to go. My emotions are a wondrous mix of sheer joy and profound relief. Joy at the unexpected, grace-filled gift that is this experience, and extraordinary relief for the silent, pent-up fears that had been asked to hold back the torrent for so long, and finally relieved of their duties.

In the aftermath, a singular, sweet pause lingers in the air, and its enchantment drapes her body like a bright shroud. Around the edges of the front curtains, outside, the day glows golden and vibrant with life. My sole thought is, *This should be shared.*

In my mind, I consciously ask myself if there is anything else that needs to be said or done before I surrender this seclusion and invite another person to enter the room with her. But almost instantly the desire to share this immense good news, this astonishing development, has me bowing to Seana's body and the photos of the saints, and propels me toward the front door.

Sweeping aside the heavy black curtain, I move from the air-conditioned semidarkness out into the brilliant, blue heat of a searing Colorado afternoon. It seems fitting that exiting the funeral parlor's chamber has converted the movie scene from black and white to technicolor, for the hues outside are eye-poppingly saturated, and the light so bright that I have to shade my eyes with both hands.

Alone at the edge of this concrete little strip mall in the dry furnace that is fall along the Front Range, a tsunami of colors and movement fans outward from where I stand. It leaves the distinct impression of fresh, new possibilities, and I recall that *possibility* was always one of Seana's favorite words.

Where are they?

At first, our three friends are nowhere in sight. Then Kelly pops up all alone from behind our car like a Jack in the Box.

Striding across the parking lot toward her, elation and wonder course through my veins, and I embrace her with a bear hug. But even though I am smiling broadly, Kelly looks doubtful and worried. Her reaction is understandable, of course. When I last left her side, we were both completely uncertain of what awaited me inside the room, and I had entered it carrying a heavy burden.

"She's beautiful!"

It's unplanned and the first thing out of my mouth. It also perfectly captures the stunning irony of my experience inside that room.

Kelly looks at me confused. These appear to be the last words she expected me to say. I can see her searching my face for the wishful thinking that she expects this to be. Kelly is a trained social worker, frequently in hospices, and knows better than most what to expect from a bereaved family member after viewing the body. But I can tell that my reaction may not be one she has seen before.

Yet the truth is that I feel extraordinary and light-hearted, and I want Kelly to feel what I am feeling. Seana was her best friend, and they already knew each other for many years before we had even met. If anyone has earned the right to experience the bliss of the pendulum swinging from devastated to deeply blessed, it is Kelly.

"Kelly, really. It's amazing. Seana is radiant!"

Now she at least gets that I am serious. Her own fears still hover near the surface, however, and I can read it in her expression. Even in my jubilance, I know better than to push her into something so deeply personal, and the ensuing silence plainly leaves it up to her whether or not to enter the parlor.

We hug one more time, and I say, "If you want to come in, you are welcome. I don't need to be alone with her anymore. We are complete." With that, I turn and reenter the viewing room.

Inside, it feels very different than only thirty minutes before. The heavy curtain on the wall of windows is slightly apart in the middle, and sunlight flashes through the gap and into the chamber.

Weightless and peaceful, I return to Seana's side and stroke her brow, sliding the headband down so that I can now see the full extent of the injury. Her right eye socket is damaged so that the eye cannot be closed. The eyeball is filmy white streaked with red, and the inner pupil is no longer round and black. A gash extends downward from the right side of her forehead, leaving a crease on that side of her face and across the eye.

Amore mio, I love you so much. Thank you for being with me, for sharing yourself so completely with me. Oh, what a lucky man am I!

It feels natural to softly sing to her, and I do. Seana always told me that my voice sounded like top-shelf brandy. Whether it was true or not doesn't matter. It's what she did.

WHENEVER I WAS rehearsing for a show, it was among the happiest times of our lives. Seana would sit sideways on the window sill working on her laptop while I rehearsed to my big band tracks in the center of the room.

Once we moved from Colorado into the cottage, this meant that we were usually about ten feet from each other. Sooner or later, the game would become her trying to distract me while I did my best to stay focused on proper vocal technique.

Seven years earlier Seana had encouraged me to form Barron's Big Band, so over the course of many such rehearsals, she came to know a number of the lyrics to the Great American Standards almost as well as I did. Thus, as I rehearsed she would pretend to be focused on her work while occasionally mouthing the lyrics. Which would have been fine, except that she could not keep a straight face and, without being too obvious, she would try to catch my attention.

She was subtle about it, and that was the fun part. As I sang, out of the corner of my eye I'd see her exaggeratedly mouthing the lyrics and looking at me out of the corner of hers. Pretending she was acting them out, her goal was to make me smile or laugh until I couldn't sing the words anymore.

Usually successful, with tremendous satisfaction she'd giggle and break into a mischievous, incandescent smile that would light up the room. Then, we'd both burst out laughing, and I would scold her appropriately for hijacking the rehearsal. Doing that, of course, delighted her immensely, and soon the game would begin all over again.

In the parlor next to her body, I hesitate for an instant, wondering if it is inappropriate to be singing. It's certainly no more so than smuggling in a candle and a lighter. Beginning very softly, quite the opposite of unsuitable, it feels absolutely guileless and touching.

> *Amore, oh oh I love you, oh oh oh oh*
> *Amore, oh oh I love you, I know you know*

A few minutes later, outside the entrance I see a shadow of movement. I know it must be Kelly, and I send a mental message. *Come in! We are here! Let's be together one last time. Share this, Kelly. You can do it. It is so beautiful!*

As if on cue, the door slowly cracks open, scattering golden light down the aisle and onto the white chairs. Backing in gently, Kelly comes through the door, head down. Cautiously, she turns herself around, glancing up and across toward where Seana and I are located. The look on her face is one of deep humility and of such vulnerability that my heart is in awe. This is not easy for her.

Feeling tremendous appreciation for her courage, I beam a smile at her that is meant to embrace her and also pull her forward toward us. Kelly smiles shyly back at me. Extinguishing the candle, I gather my backpack while still softly singing the improvised part of the tune from "Volare."

Kelly takes a deep breath, looks directly at Seana's body, and walks slowly forward. Instinctively, I make way for her and slowly leave the chamber to them—two old friends, together one last time.

Once outside, the heat and sun are like a catalyst whose thermodynamics bond my shirt to my skin within minutes. Eventually our other two friends emerge from the nearby park, and I share with them my experience. I try to convey the overarching beauty that I know is present in the room, but they, too, are unsure and unsettled by my tale. However, the lightness of my state of mind and heart cannot be mistaken, and eventually they are knocking softly on the funeral parlor door seeking an audience with Seana's body.

Inside the chamber, I quietly sit myself a few rows back and watch it all unfold. It is an extraordinary sight to witness. Individually and as a collective, they walk to and fro about her remains placing flowers around her head and offering prayers. Observing the three of them feels like watching sunlight spread across a field at dawn. The longer they interact with Seana's body, the lighter they become.

As they finish, the room that I first entered over an hour before is completely gone. In fact, nothing is the same, nor am I the same one who entered the chamber. The gift that this is cannot be exaggerated, and a feeling of spaciousness and freedom permeates my vision, every sound I hear, the fragrance in the room, and even the taste in my mouth.

DAYS SEVEN & EIGHT

17. Online Ohana

THE FOLLOWING DAY, I am prepared for a second phone call with Swamiji. Only six days ago, when we first spoke after Seana's accident, I was in a very different place. Today, rather than focusing on my own emotions, the goal is to better understand how to share with others about the thirteenth day.

All over the internet and the world, it turns out, people are asking how to participate in sending Seana into the light on the final day, and I am hoping my friend the monk can help me get clearer about how to support them.

"What grace, Swamiji, and deep transformation. I feel it so many different ways. It's just crazy."

"It's amazing you can be open to that, you know. It's a compliment of the sadhana you've done for years that you don't just collapse. Which is understandable too, but that you have that muscle to open."

"It's the teachings. Like what a gift! Deeply beautiful, except when it's so painful. Multiple times today, I'm in deep tears. But it's all love."

"Yeah, I think that's going to happen for a while. You don't want to push that away. It's a tribute to what you two had together."

"Well, thank you for being such a willing participant. The level of impact my wife had on people around the globe is stunning. They're asking for information and guidance about the thirteenth day and what happens to her after that."

"I think there is a merging back into the energy body and into the light. And at a certain point the being probably goes to another realm where they continue their evolution. It's my conviction that even there you can communicate with them. But, in essence, even the soul is temporary. The light is one's true nature.

"And then there's a moment when you wake up to your greater soul's arc, lifetime to lifetime, where you've been the daughter in this life, the father in the last ... That's the way I understand it.

"She'll wake up to the light of her soul. There can still be sending blessings and invoking their presence, but in a way where you honor them as light. You're not trying to pull them back into a particular form or into a particular way of being. You want them to experience that expansion of the light."

Hoping to get as clear as possible, I asked, "So, years from now, most people would be left with the idea of merging into the light and then going into a different realm based on their samskaras? Maybe I'll just call them patterns, so others understand."

"The place where they'll learn," Swamiji emphasized. "Where they'll be filled with God's love, too. When you truly love the person as coequals and growing together, you relish that form. And at the same time, you love that person so much, you want them to rise up into the supreme love. Because both of you, that's where you're going together.

"For that reason, I think to invoke or send love is different from something like, 'We won't let you go.' When a person has that emotional neediness, it's almost like a contraction that would hold the spirit, and because the one departing is also worried about you, your energy holds her. She's concerned about you.

"But when you say, 'You were the very gift of my life. You supported me in growing, and I send you blessings ...' You could say what she meant to you and then invite other people to share what she meant to them."

"That's helpful, Swamiji, because there are people all around the world that are looking for a clearer understanding of how to express their deep love for Seana on that thirteenth day."

"It's going to be people from different traditions, right? And you're going to be the host?"

"No. There are so many people around the globe who've been moved by Seana. I don't know most of them, but I've seen them asking on social media. I'll just leave a post."

"I think the idea is to send blessings that she can merge with the light and love of God, rather than saying, 'Let go.' You could model it, 'This is what you meant to my life, how you uplifted and inspired me.' Then everybody can do it in their own heart."

Already, a rough idea of what I wanted to say was forming in my mind.

"So, when do you go to Hawaii?" Swamiji asked. "I remember so many afternoons when we would meet up there. We always connected somehow over many years. It was really very interesting. We'd see you there on the beach with your surfboard ready to go and looking out at the islands—*and beyond*. It was like an eternal moment of time where the ocean represented the future and the journey, and who knew what lay in store?

"And that takes you into a kind of cosmic realm, like little did we know that you would meet someone there and you would go on this journey, and you would return. I think it could be really beautiful to be there and also nurtured by Lanikai. To thank God and friends there."

"My plan is to go there on the thirteenth day before sunrise. Every time Seana and I would go to Hawaii, we'd go to that spot at sunrise on the beach and renew our vows. She would paddle her longboard out into the ocean toward the Mokulua Islands, and as the sun rose she'd put her arms outstretched and invoke the blessings of the universe. I'd be on the beach chanting the Guru Gita. So, I plan to be on our spot where we met and were married."

"Have you ever read the *Yoga Vasistha*? I mean your journey reminds me of it. You know, how someone goes into a dream, lives for a whole lifetime, and they wake up a moment later in the same place?"

This stopped me. Though I had read the book several times, there was something else here. With interest, I asked, "What about my story makes you feel that?"

"Well, you were there, and you've gone into this marriage and journey together, and now you come back to the same place."

"Oh my god."

"You know what I mean? But different. And it's like you think it's some fantasy, but we each go through these journeys which don't leave any traces, in some ways like the ocean. They come, they are very real, and then we move on. And this is what at the end is called our life's journey, and who could have imagined it? It's dreamlike and very real at the same time.

"I keep seeing us there on the beach. Your journey happens

from there, and you come back with this amazing vision. Who would know what joy, what pain, would be waiting for you."

"Swamiji, I'm beyond grateful for the karma that you and I have together."

"I really felt for you! And I felt like we met for some reason, that there's some arc there. I'll keep offering prayers up to the thirteenth day, and I'm glad you're taking care of yourself. That's really important, and that's important for Seana, too. One of the most important things is that she sees that you've got your spiritual support and you will carry on."

18. Amid Seana's Belongings

L AST NIGHT WAS a rough one. There are so many chambers in the heart, and the wall that came down was of a life without Seana, of loneliness, and for the delight and play that she brought to every hour.

It may also have something to do with the fact that I am staying in the same room that she occupied for her last few weeks and final morning. It was from here that she got into our Prius and began her drive toward Boulder, eventually choosing to travel via Highway 66. I probably should have expected that sleeping in the same bed surrounded by her belongings might create some issues.

Ironically, I literally asked for this. Before leaving the cottage for our friends' home in Colorado, I spoke to Sharon and asked her to please leave the room exactly as Seana had left it. *Touch nothing.* I can't remember why I chose this, but I do recall being very clear about it. For some reason, I gave almost no thought to what it might be like to stay in the room where she spent her final days.

After the call with Swamiji yesterday, I spent most of the afternoon and evening quietly bundled up in this little basement guest room surrounded by Seana's belongings. To move about, I had to gingerly step over piles of her folded clothing and neatly organized stacks of personal items that had been laid out across the carpet, each still awaiting its turn to go into a suitcase for her flight home.

Nor could I bring myself to move any of those things more than a few inches from where I found them. I would pick things up, look at them or read something she had written on a sticky note, and then place it right back where I had found it. I simply could not fathom where it should go. In the trash? Into storage? To Goodwill? It simply took too much life-energy to think about, much less do something with.

In fact, why was I even here? Hadn't I needed every bit of last week to recover a semblance of inner balance within the safe haven of the cottage? Yet for some reason I chose to place myself right back into the hottest part of the fire. Why did I do that?

Soon, it wasn't long before thoughts like *Seana was a radiant being* and *I will never again know another one like her* had me doubled over, and then the *never agains* began to pour out of me like a burst levee in a floodplain. I just kept seeing her joy. One after another, the images would not stop coming, and they stole away my fragile truce like a battalion of soldiers rolling into a conquered city.

And finally, in this tiny, bitterly cold room, it was her playfulness and rare appreciation for life that shattered my heart that evening. To understand with absolute certainty that I would never again experience firsthand her infectious, childlike power to infuse moments with sheer delight was unbearable, and a physical pain tore through my body as if it was the first time.

With nowhere to put the mass of affection and longing that was surging powerfully through me, intense love flipped to its antipode and became boundless grief gushing out of me like water from broken pipes one floor up. And then, for one more night, into the abyss of *never again* we went together, my beloved and I.

DAYS NINE & TEN

19. Tapasya

AFTER SPENDING MY final hours surrounded by thirteen of our most intimate friends, I left Colorado like an arrow shot from an archer's bow. Something was awaiting me in Hawaii, and though I could not know what it was, imagining that it had something to do with the thirteenth day was more than enough.

Thirty-five thousand feet above the Pacific Ocean and somewhere about halfway to Oahu, I remembered that, three days before she was killed and at the end of our nightly phone conversation, out of the blue Seana had asked me, "What one thing would you want me to remember tonight before I go to sleep?"

This was an unusual question. In fact, this was the only time she'd ever asked it before ending one of our phone conversations. Immediately, my response came, "I would want you to remember your purpose for being alive."

Carried away by the rawness of this recollection, for a long time I floated in the vast hemisphere of blue outside the airplane window and amid memories of how we first met and fell so deeply in love. Eventually, I found myself contemplating the fifth of the seven wedding vows that we'd spoken on Lanikai Beach. "I will support and celebrate the fulfillment of your life's purpose, both inner and outer."

The root of the Sanskrit word, tapasya, means "to heat," and in sadhana (the spiritual journey) tapasya refers to the burning away of the mental and emotional impurities from our past, which get stored like seeds in the subtle body, the realm of our thoughts and feelings.

Burned into my memory was the time I created an entire poster of Seana's unacceptable behaviors. To someone unfamiliar with our troubles, and if not for the seriousness of the crossroads in our lives that it represented, the web of arrows and colorful markers might have appeared like a child's treasure map. Except that, of course, when you followed it in closer to the larger words in capital letters, RIGID—CONTROLLING—INFLEXIBLE, its meaning became very clear.

For seven years, I had used the challenges in our relationship as fuel for the fire of my spiritual practices. And boy, did I need the practice. Not because Seana was terribly difficult to live with, although even superheroes can get overwhelmed at times by what they see reflected back at them through their life-partners. But rather, because most of these troubles I had created all on my own, samskaras patiently awaiting their turn in line like waves stacked out to the horizon. My journals were absolutely overflowing with years of effort to reflect, reframe, and restore the inner balance that kept getting submerged in the chaos of the outer world.

Perhaps Seana's observation of me is true. *Freedom is your core value.* At times, she spoke these words to me like a true best friend (which she was) and at others in total exasperation (which I often merited). For someone whose principal samskaras were often related to the fear of domination, liberation was not only the root of my deepest longing, but also a reflection of my starkest fear—having no control.

As my spouse, Seana witnessed me acting out both extremes far too often. Unfortunately, negative hardwired patterns masquerade *as us,* and a large part of my struggle was spent sorting through the conflicting evidence and trying to understand, *who am I?*

My samskaras made me dance like a puppet over a hot fire, and while I was under their spell, I blamed my feelings either on the outside world or the nearest person. For me, that person was often Seana. Why? Ultimately, because it's just so much easier than taking responsibility, and because the ego absolutely hates to be wrong.

Until now, the one thing that had always stopped me from leaving Seana was that whenever I was seized by a particularly deep pattern, I was not sure if I could live without her. Over the years, every time I caught myself on the verge of speaking the unspeakable words, I would carefully examine what life would be like afterwards, and as a result, step back from the precipice, chastened. Fortunately, over the years I learned that this moment never lied.

Yet this time, as I contemplated the severity and depth of the impasse, I was compelled to test out that imaginary future repeatedly. I sat for extended periods trying to journal or chant from the core of what hurt most, as well as from the center of the *me* who would have to live with the consequences of a separation or divorce. In spite of that, the deadlock—that tight slab of granite-like pride inside my heart as solid as the middle of a mountain—remained as unmoved as ever.

As I told John during one of our numerous phone calls over this extremely difficult period, "I have no other choice. I barely recognize myself. Her inflexibility is killing me off, and I can't continue like this anymore."

This was not news to John. Since he first married us on Lanikai Beach, he was the recipient of several similar calls over the years. John was not a pastor, just a wise and trusted friend, and in the past he had always been able to help me see something that I was missing.

So much so that "Call John" became one of Seana's go-to responses whenever a particularly divisive issue repeated its cycle. But after a while, it got to the point where she'd used it too many times. I remember once in the midst of a heated discussion in our kitchen, even before Seana could finish saying those words to me, I responded, "I am *not* calling John about this." At which point we both burst into laughter at the humor and irony of it.

Nonetheless, given the unacceptable and stagnant nature of what I described to him on the phone, this time John had agreed with me. Change was necessary for both our sakes. Thus, as Seana and I approached the day for our big meeting, instead of hollow and afraid as I had experienced so many times before when I'd made empty threats, I felt prepared and resolved. Having reached the ultimate tipping point, I was finally willing to do the unthinkable. If nothing changed, I was going to leave our marriage and Seana behind.

Nor was it a secret to Seana that I harbored these intense, unresolved feelings. First, because we had been actively engaging, discussing, and in counseling for these very issues for years, but especially over the last few months. And second, because after completing the poster with its diagram of evidence and blame, I taped it to the wall in our meditation room.

Looking back, this seems like a dramatic and even comical thing to have done, but at the time I was deadly serious, and it had the desired effect. With a loud and explosive shot across the bow of our marriage, the poster on the wall conveyed my message: Things must change, because change is coming, regardless.

And thus, approximately two weeks later we met in our meditation room to settle it, once and for all.

OUR MEDITATION ROOM was a fairly sizeable space located in the basement of our even more sizable Colorado home. Every day, some combination of chanting, journaling, *hatha yoga*, and meditation took place inside its peach-colored walls. Through the years, whenever one of us felt the relationship was truly at risk, it would metamorphose into a sanctuary where we could meet and speak freely. Without this structure to support us, our most difficult discussions would have simply proved too volatile, and things might have been said that, once heard, could never be taken back.

That morning, standing side-by-side before the puja, rays of light filtered in through the small basement window. Angling in and downward, brilliant specks of dust floated through the sunshine and crisscrossed our bodies like fireflies. On the puja, Baba, Gurumayi, and Nityananda sat side-by-side with the Dalai Lama and Lama Tsultrim. Into that stillness we lit candles and waved incense before the pictures of our teachers.

The meditation room altar was a good metaphor for how we approached our different spiritual paths as a married couple. It showed our deep, mutual appreciation and respect for each other. In this way, I had gone with her to visit the Dalai Lama when he came to town, and she took a Siddha Yoga Shaktipat Intensive with me.

As we took our places in the middle of the room, instead of facing each other, we sat back-to-back. Thus, each could speak freely without having to see the other's facial reaction. Over many years, this system had helped keep judgments at bay, giving us the buffer we needed to work through some extremely challenging issues.

With meditation cushions and blankets in place, our spines gradually came to rest against one another's. Just as this positioning had done so many times before, like a mnemonic cue, it reminded me of our purpose for being here—to bring out our personal and collective best. The spreading warmth of our joined bodies infused the moment with a deep sense of respect, and even though I was steeling myself for a challenging session, I knew that no unkind words would be exchanged.

For the next hour, we spoke respectfully and even eloquently without interrupting one another. What each felt needed to be heard was expressed to its fullest extent without interruption, and though these things were unpleasant to say out loud, we both made frequent efforts to repeat back what we understood the other person to have said before responding to it.

Nevertheless, as the discussion wore on, it became apparent that we were being inexorably drawn toward completion without consensus. It felt similar to being sucked around the rim of a drain where the whirling vortex holds everything in place by centrifugal force. Neither one of us could move inward even a little bit from our position. And even though we were sitting back-to-back, it began to appear painfully obvious that our hearts were still worlds apart.

With this intuition, a subtle but deep sorrow slowly began to infuse everything that we had left to say, because nothing could hide the fact that we were at a standoff unlike any before.

I made another attempt to reach out, but without releasing my grip on any demands. Energetically, this was not a recipe for success.

"Seana, our wedding vow to support and celebrate the fulfillment of each other's life purpose, both inner and outer, is the hub of all our vows. To support one another in that way requires absolute fluidity and flexibility on our part because each of our life purposes is so high and requires commitment and faith, as it must.

"It also shows that we are different. We have two distinctly different life purposes, and the support and path toward their fulfillment will look very different for each of us. And because there is nothing higher than fulfilling our life purposes, they impact all our choices and structures as a married couple. This was and is my purpose for marrying you, Seana. That we walk together, side by side, toward their fulfillment, while also aware and honoring how different they may appear."

Softly, she replied, "I thought that merging was our purpose."

With those few words, Seana hit the bullseye of what had remained buried and unspoken until now. In her voice, I could unmistakably hear fatigue as well as a deep sadness, as if she was on the verge of letting go.

"Beloved love," she continued, "*is* choosing that human love is an expression of the divine, of God, and that we are in committed relationship and practicing sadhana for the fulfillment of that. There's not a final attainment, but a developing of our practice."

Although I heard the power in what she was saying and may have even recognized it as true, I could not keep my mind from being drawn back to its chief complaint—how rigid the walls of our lives had become.

Why do we have to schedule every aspect of life, every minute of every day?

For me, those requirements, and especially her inflexibility with them, eclipsed most of the spontaneity and joy out of life. And as our marriage continued, I was finding that I needed more and more time to replenish my inner resources, and with greater frequency. In my heart, I knew that if nothing changed, I had no chance. I would not make it, nor would I ever be who I needed to be for either one of us.

When you're drowning, very few things are in your mind. Having almost gone down in large surf on at least two occasions, I recognized the similarities. In that crisis, three things share center stage: a feeling of desperation, an all-encompassing fear of death, and—for getting out of the life-threatening situation—a shot of adrenaline.

Although the last two ingredients were missing, I recognized quite clearly that I was desperate and drowning, though not in a way that I had ever before experienced. Unlike the sudden violence and power of the ocean, this was a slow and steady drowning. It felt like I had been drifting further and further out to sea for a very long time and I could see no recognizable landmarks in any direction.

Seana had been quiet for some time. Outside, the wind was gently rustling through the Chinese elms, making that swish-swish-swishing sound that can be so deeply relaxing. It was a beautiful day out there. Inside the room, sunlight and the dancing shadows of tree branches and their leaves flickered on the walls in perfect detachment, offering reminders that nothing is set in stone.

One of our most treasured marriage vows was "I will meet what arises with playfulness, wonder, and ease." Seana has always proven to be infinitely better at this one than I—and before it grew too late, I think if I could have, I would have summoned the willpower to rise to it and turn this train around. But sadly, that was far beyond the realm of my capacity, and I knew it. I had prepared for battle with a daunting adversary, not for compromise. There was nothing to do but recognize its impossibility, and indeed just how late it had become.

Perhaps Seana was expecting me to respond, but there was nothing left to say. Or possibly she, too, had become aware of the impassable divide between us and that our time was running out. Maybe she was just winding up like a clock or a pitcher on the mound, and using that high-powered intellect and finely tuned heart to reach a conclusion. If so, I sensed that it would be her final one of the day.

It's ironic how your own name can shake you enough that a hairline crack in your armor appears, where before, nothing was there. And though it would not make itself known for many hours, it set into motion invisible processes along with an unexpected outcome.

"Faith in beloved love creates the opportunity to love again and again," she said. "Merging with God is merging with each other. That's what I thought we were marrying for, Barron."

Hearing her say my name out loud had the effect of waking me just enough so that one last time I remembered to pause before responding. In that brief interval, I clearly saw that I was being neither who I'd declared that I would always be for her, nor living up to the vows that had gotten us this far. From somewhere high above the room and my body, detached from my judgments, I vaguely understood that her words were the very ones that I myself should have been saying.

What I said next was, by necessity, only a reiteration of an earlier statement, but it came out more like a closing argument. Hidden inside the words was also a plea, but I had struck too hard and strayed too far to be rescued now.

"Seana, I have given everything I have over and over and over. This path we've been walking together has taken every ounce of my stamina and courage. For me, there's nothing more important than fulfilling one's life purpose. It's central to everything."

"Yes, I've always known that it feels that way to you," she replied. "You see it as high and narrow, but I see the path as wide, flowing, and everywhere. You don't see me the way you see Baba and Gurumayi, even though I was in your vision at Gold Lake. But I see you as divine, and I bow to your feet. The heartbreak is that you do not."

She must have been aware of the power of her words because she paused, allowing them to land. It was as if she had pulled the pin on a hand grenade and lightly tossed it over her shoulder. Her words—and above all, the aura of heartbreak, loss, and longing in them—fell in my lap, exploding deep inside me like nothing else had that morning. The stinging, burning away of unseen layers from many lifetimes of selfishness would certainly leave a scar. Once again, I was grateful that she could not see my face. Then, she got right to the heart of the matter as only Seana could.

"The last two years I have been living on a precipice between life and death. I almost bled to death with colitis! Your family! Multiple Sclerosis! But all of the things that supported me—you, nature, community with others—suddenly those were not available to me anymore. My supports were gone, and I had to focus my energy on just surviving. So, I had less to bring to us.

"And my love language is service," she continued, "so having to ask you for help, it felt like you do not love me. *But all is available*

… Supreme bliss is available in every moment. That is present for me. But it's not present for you.

"Try to remember that at first you didn't even want to go to your yoga center in Boulder, but *I* encouraged you. You asked me to do a Shaktipat Intensive with you, and even though I had no interest in doing it, I did that to have a deeper connection with you and to encourage the fulfillment of your life's purpose.

"The heartbreak is that you are not in a place of seeing *me* as divine—as Baba, Gurumayi, and Seana. Over the years, even after you promised that you wouldn't make me responsible for your well-being and happiness, you've blamed me for your unhappiness. I only ever wanted to give you what you needed. That is my habit, and it's mine to own. But along the way I lost myself and my vision. I tried to compensate for your unending dissatisfaction, for your family's negative views of me, and I tried to always believe in us."

Her disappointment and frustration plainly evident, I could sense that she was inching toward some irreconcilable verdict.

"I thought I was marrying all our letters, our communicating through sensual love, what we shared at the start through word and touch."

Even before she said it, I knew all was lost—no possibility of resolution. At the edge of the cliff, but no longer wavering, she spoke her final words.

"But just like you, I'm no longer willing to settle for less."

Within moments, Seana exited the meditation room.

ALONE NOW, THERE was a stillness. The late morning sun was still shooting shafts of gold through the basement window and onto the carpet. Along with my thoughts, aerosols drifted aimlessly through the light, visible for a short while only to disappear, never to be seen again.

Soundlessly ricocheting off the walls, a river of melancholy rippled its way through the room, pooling around the corners in eddies of sorrow. I knew she was done, and that perhaps we were too.

From somewhere deep within me arose the subtle vibrations of words that I first heard inside my head when I was a boy and the home where we lived, once a beacon of love, had become lightless. At times, we couldn't pay all our bills, and many of the lights were kept out to conserve energy.

I remember the feeling of walking through the house after dusk and having to pass through so many shadows just to get to the kitchen. By then, sickness and mental disease were not only in my mother, but had begun to spread its depressive, subtler markings into the psyches of each of us three children—and perhaps, by the end, into my beautiful grandfather too.

Traveling the great distance of the ellipse, the reverberations of those words now returned across time and space to the meditation room and closed the curve.

This is how it really is ... this is how it really is ... and this is how it always will be.

I REMEMBER A particularly sunless season as a young teen where it seemed almost every night I would come out of my room, cross the living room, and creep down the three stairs just outside my mother's bedroom door. Silently, I would pause there to listen in the dark.

Hearing nothing, I would softly reach for the shiny gold-colored handle. I knew that if it turned even slightly, it was unlocked, and then I would noiselessly go back to bed. But if it was locked, it meant things were not right with her, and I feared almost any dark event might be going on inside her room. In those cases, I would knock loudly.

"Mama? Are you all right? Can I please come in? The door is locked, and you're scaring me."

Of the many things that can happen to you as a boy when your mother chooses the wrong second husband, a violent man thirteen years younger who himself grew up amid spousal abuse, the recurring scene above is but one image from a multi-faceted stone, just one more detail in a cascading string of sorrows that descend with unmatched precision to remodel your life.

Another outcome is that the priceless family that surrounds you, raised in love and as an expression of love, all become vulnerable and anxious. Beaten up emotionally and physically too, it only leaves for debate which is worse—the obviously visible scars or the longer-lasting, undetectable ones.

Over the latter half of that man's eleven years with us, there were weeks or months when he would leave the house, swearing at us in anger that he wasn't ever coming back, and the whole family and the house itself felt haunted at all hours because we knew he would.

One final after-effect, for there are far too many to visit here (and calling up the past without a clear intention to let it go is, to put it lightly, disadvantageous), is that after a few years of this I became a teenager sleeping with a baseball bat by my door and filling the back alley between my bedroom and our wooden fence outside with a hundred carefully placed, tall, empty glass candles. The supply was endless as, over time, my beautiful but overwhelmed mother burned them like a chain smoker in hopes of keeping the darkness and depression from consuming her.

Thus, my hypothesis went, if *that one* should try to sneak back into the house without us knowing, he'd stumble over the impenetrable lines of foot-high glass soldiers and the warning signals would sound, calling me into battle.

In this way, those candles enjoyed a renaissance of sorts. Once lit for my mother's prayers, they attained a rebirth into a second life as my crude-but-effective alarm system. Over the years, there were indeed a few times in the middle of the night when the first row was broken, to be followed by total silence. So, who knows? Perhaps they were the answer to one of her prayers. I do know that they helped me sleep at night.

Him ... Rodger. I still don't like to say his name out loud or even think it. It leaves a bitter, acrid taste, even though I understand that he did his best and served his purpose. After all, someone had to play that karmic role for the learning to occur.

But not until adulthood did I come to understand that cycles of abuse do not end themselves without immense willpower and professional support, neither of which he had. For abuse begets abuse in unseen and unfathomable ways. *That one* grew up in a house where his father beat his mother, and nobody in that house, or era, ever said anything about it. Thus, the cycle was perpetuated because he was a bully, a coward who berated and beat women, and occasionally old men and children.

Though my mother was his main target, my sisters and grandpa also took his fire. But I never did. He never laid a finger on me, except that by my seventeenth year—when at last he disappeared for good—my mind was a mass of invisible scars with his fingerprints all over them, waves of samskaras awaiting their appointed times and lined up inside my mind like corduroy.

Imagine then how deep the hardwired grooves must go for my dear mother who (even after years of targeted abuse)—one sunny

California morning when *that one* was finally ready to leave for good—wept bitterly and grabbed onto his legs so that he had to shuffle sideways like a sand crab across the driveway to get to his car.

I remember watching this scene from about ten yards away in utter disbelief. In an image that was among the most disturbing and confusing of my young life, here was a man who had abused our family, and primarily her. Yet after years of exhaustive efforts (particularly mine) to rid our family of his foul shadow, she could not let him leave once and for all.

Flabbergasted, I asked her, "Why Mama? Why can't you just let him go?"

Kneeling on the cement with her arms still grasping onto one of his legs, she turned her head back toward me. The look in her eyes was of a torment beyond my ability to comprehend. "Because *I love him*, Barron," she replied.

20. Fearless Love

A s a fourth- and fifth-grade school teacher, one of the things I enjoyed teaching children about was Pangaea, the supercontinent that forms and splits apart on the surface of the Earth every several hundred million years.

Once, I blew up a blue balloon and painted one single land-mass onto its surface in thickened paint. Coloring it in and with hairline cracks along the continental borders, when it was inflated, it split itself off into the seven continents, all spreading outward until eventually they assumed roughly their modern-day posi-tions. This took several attempts, but it was well worth it.

Later, when we were discussing the theory of Pangaea and its critical role in the evolutionary history of our planet, I pulled it out for effect as a fully inflated bit of realia. We were at the part where we learn that every year the continents are actually inching back toward each other to eventually reform again into one mas-sive supercontinent. Right then, I began to deflate the balloon a little bit at a time. Slowly, like pieces of a planetary puzzle, the colorful mudball continents all shrunk back together into one landmass. The class let out an audible gasp. It was awesome.

In one sense, the event in the meditation room with Seana was my Pangaea. But instead of taking three-hundred million years, it was happening all in one day. In my own evolution, the question at that point, literally and figuratively, seemed unambiguous. Are you coming together or splitting apart? It was all about direction and intent.

According to the plethora of journal entries that I was now sifting through like the white sand on Lanikai Beach, this state of latent tension had been part of my personal history for a very long time. Here on these pages was the radiant heat of thermal stress, a written record of all those life-lessons, as well as a seemingly endless supply of fuel for burning.

In fact, the intensity and frequency were something that had almost driven Seana away multiple times, especially at the beginning of our relationship. It was as if the metronome of my life had been set at an elevated rate, and the rhythmic swing of its pendulum was never more active than during my years with Seana.

I also discovered evidence of something that I desperately needed to be reminded of at this moment. My cycles have neither been pretty nor always ended well, but I have never given up. Already since this morning's incident in the meditation room, there had been a subtle, yet obvious, shift. Despite the fact that on the surface I may have appeared relatively unscathed, in truth it had shaken me to my foundations. It was only a matter of time before the cracks became broader fissures and began to show themselves.

Later that afternoon, I sent a message to John in Hawaii— Urgent. Can we please talk again ASAP?

When I finally got him on the phone, I found myself wondering how he would react to the bad news. His earlier support had meant a lot to me, but in the aftermath of this morning, I was uncertain about absolutely everything and openly searching for clues.

"So, how did it go, buddy?"

"Not well. It may be the end of us," I replied.

"Really?" John seemed genuinely surprised.

"Yes, she would not move one iota from her position."

"Well, what did she say?"

"Basically that I am creating all this, and that only I can solve it."

"Hmm ... Are you?" The sound of his voice left me disconcerted, and I could tell that he was obviously not in the same place as our last conversation.

"Well," I replied, "it is possible, I suppose." I hadn't expected him to capitulate so quickly, and it unnerved me.

"Do you think I'm wrong to demand change?" I asked.

There was a long pause on the other end of the line. When at last he finally spoke, I could tell that my dear friend had made up his mind.

"Here's what I think, buddy. It's tapasya!

"That's all this has ever been. *Extremely intense tapasya!* You're doing battle with the samskaras, and this has all been coming up so that you could see them, experience that karma, and burn it off. It feels like you're fighting for your life right now, because you've got them on the ropes!"

John laughed. "It's nothing but old, old patterns that you chose to work through a long time ago. Just finish them off and move on." He seemed delighted with his breakthrough.

"You want to know what I think?" he asked.

"I think Seana is the fuel—the vehicle for your growth," he said. "And her behavior, all that stuff that you can't stand, is the *tapasya*. It's the gift, buddy! It's just that it's burning really bad right now, and so you're having second thoughts." I could hear him chuckling in the background as he said this.

"But you have to keep moving forward. *It's who you are.* It's why you're here, and it's what you've always prayed to the guru for. You want to be free. So, be free. See it all as tapasya and be free."

When we finally hung up, I was devastated, but in the best possible way. Not just because his words felt true and right, but because he, like Seana, was calling to a part of me that I had left for dead. With an unstoppable chain reaction, a series of reversals had been set in motion.

That one word, *tapasya*, had tossed the lie high up into the air, and with just one more deep cut, mysterious and razor-sharp, it was going to land on its opposite side.

HOURS LATER, IN the sacred space of the meditation room, I was surrounded. Encircled by my computer, journals, and a box of tissues—it looked as though I was under attack by a foreign flotilla. But these were friendlies, allies come to my aid when I needed them most. With their help, I began to search through the abundant archives of the earliest correspondence that Seana and I had shared.

They did not disappoint. One by one, the long strings of emails and messages presented themselves before me like lanterns in a dark forest. Although there were too many to possibly take in at once, reading the first few had the same effect as a bracing splash of ice-cold water. Written in the language of love, our communications pointed to the unmistakable recognition of our limitless possibilities. To revisit them was a gripping act of remembrance and all-consuming, like breathing in a familiar, dense fragrance that carries you back in time to pivotal moments and forgotten feelings.

The more I read, the more the optics of the morning's discussion began to take on an encouraging light in stark contrast to my actual memory of the experience. Its effect was thaumaturgic and miraculous.

Imagine a bone-weary traveler passing through a relentlessly dense woodland over a long period of time, only to emerge all at once into an enormous, bright clearing. I'd almost forgotten what one looked like. Wonder-stricken, before my very eyes sublime visions of who we were for each other flickered in the distance like fireflies, *and I remembered.*

Fearless love, we had called it.

I was her *Efil*—Extreme Fearless Italian Lover, and she was my *Signorina Bav*—Born Again Virgin. She was so funny and steadfast about that, and it took me so long to get her. And then once I got her ... What happened? When had I lost that longing to serve, to honor her, to walk the path together and bring out our best in the process?

With the inner chamber now breached, there was little left in me to stem the flow, and even less desire to do so. In my search, I encountered letters that were written with near poetic devotion. Like a peal of bells ringing out their signal, the words and their intent contained a faithfulness and fervor that was indisputable.

The more I read, the clearer it shone forth—the unique beauty and rare opportunity that comes into existence when we are together. It felt akin to stumbling upon a lost world. I rediscovered the pure gold of fearlessness, declarations of love, and the mutual desire to uplift and benefit others. And I came across my Self.

Dazed, I sat there on the floor staring at the screen. From the center of my chest a point of warmth slowly spread outward until my entire body filled up with raw emotion like a parched, dry thing that has been cracked and ridden with dust—and at last the rains have come.

Who am I? Where did I go? Gathering momentum, the realization steadily expanded into a flash flood, sweeping away everything in its path. Nothing had roots deep enough to withstand the deluge.

"What happened to me?" I said out loud. "I don't understand, anymore!"

Hand over mouth in disbelief, the immensity of the loss struck me with its full force, and along with that came a deep sadness once I understood that I had taken down my best friend too.

Where did that selflessness go? How did selfishness come to replace it?

Tears fell from my eyes and from the center of my being. Coursing through my body, the sting of remorse wrung out every last drop of emotion and longing. Again and again, it washed me clean, leaving me dry and empty like a discarded shell with no living creature inside.

I'm so sorry, Amore. I'm so deeply sorry.

Please help me, Gurudev!

Why is this so hard? Why can't I do it? Please help me!

Then I found her declaration. It was the crest jewel in a crown already crowded with gems, and I recognized this one correspondence as *the* moment. Her vow of fearlessness. Her leap of faith. And the beauty of its eloquence, the evident courage within its words, and the purity of the spirit who had written them broke me into thousands of tiny, unrecognizable pieces.

Just as I had lost myself somewhere along the way, I lost myself now in embers and ashes. Her words made me question everything that I thought I had understood about what *absolutely had to change in her*, and what it was that *I could not possibly continue with any longer.*

God, I am dramatic—so damn intense. It's a miracle that she stayed with me this long. She must be fireproof.

And yet such a conundrum! At times she was the fiercest warrior and an unwavering stand for all she valued. Yet that beautiful one could also be so fragile, a little girl who—when inconsolably saddened by the immense suffering she perceived in the world—had only one wish, to be held tightly and allowed to fully experience without judgment whatever she was feeling. She had only ever asked to be "heard and known" (her words), to be loved exactly as she was in every moment. And I failed.

It was just as she said this morning. "I see you as divine. The heartbreak is that you do not."

What were all those years of spiritual practice for, anyway? In addition to liberation, weren't they also intended for just such a moment, just such a trial? And I failed. I failed my Amore.

Gathering me up in as firm a hold as any rapidly rising swell at sea ever had, waves of ineffable sadness poured through me. I grabbed the box of tissues left from our talk, using them like towels to staunch the flow. One by one, each tissue became soaked like something forgotten and left out in the rain, little balls of white gathering around me on the carpet like a flock of sheep or drenched clouds so heavy that they needed to rest on land.

In my mind, I heard the words, *I am hopeless*, but they felt hollow. Once seen, cycles wind down, even samskaras older than time. It was enough, and no more good was going to come of replaying it. At last, the inner chatter stopped.

In front of me, my computer screen had gone dark. Touching a key on the keyboard, I looked down at her words, her declaration to the universe of fearless, beloved love. Unlike my approach to sadhana, it was a statement of who she *is*, not who she hoped to one day become. She was already living it, breathing it, and hoping that I might wake up in time to share it with her.

Even with her flaws. This last thought made me smile. *Her huge flaws.* And then genuine laughter. Seana was far from perfect—but what a beauty.

Looking down at the words again, at her soul's proclamation, it was as though what she'd written a few months after we'd first met was penned only this afternoon.

> *Barone,*
>
> *Fear was almost overwhelming last night for me, and it took everything I had not to give in to its power in the face of your power. It took everything I had to stay with you, and I feel like crying from this sense of narrowly escaping severe harm. Your intensity last night was very, very hard for me to be with in a loving and open way … today I am spent from what it took, and am reeling from the fear that I felt in the presence of it.*
>
> *How can it be that, as self-aware as you are, you do not know how powerful you are? I'm breathing hard emotionally. I'm a bit shaky. I want to cry from relief that I, and we, survived, that I didn't make a misstep that set you in full harmful motion and trigger you to leave, be done with me, dismiss me. I need to breathe deeply into trust. I feel like my heart needs a hug and some reassurance that I'm safe, and will always be safe with you.*
>
> *AND THEN I KNOW THAT EVEN IF YOU WERE TO*

LEAVE SOME DAY, I WOULD NEVER TRADE THE FREE FALL FOR ANYTHING … that it is a part of my purpose to fully experience and express all that is possible for love, and that my fullest capacity for loving and living is brought forth with you, and that you are my true partner. May this always be … I do not need any promises from you. I know that for me this is right and good and true, and I will live it fully and fearlessly for all of our time together.

Like a tremendous landslide where half the mountain falls away, with one sudden collapse the long recorded history of Seana's unbearable words and actions slipped from view. In the gaping hole it left behind, I understood. She had found me again.

For it's one of the truest threads of my life story that my teachers' words keep returning to pull me out of whatever abyss I have fallen into. I'm like a child who does not look before stepping and winds up in all sorts of trouble. Quite simply, I'd gotten myself lost in a dream that became a nightmare. And Seana, who can't bear for me to suffer even in a dream, enters it and calls to me.

OBVIOUSLY, THERE WAS a massive mess to be cleaned up. The debris from the nearly fatal roadside collision that was now strewn across our lives must be attended to without delay. I know that sounds incredibly ironic to say, given how this story began. Nevertheless, it was true, and I knew exactly where to start.

My first act would be to tear down the poster. Standing before it one last time, I reread the words, those curious letters and symbols that can be twisted to mean almost anything. Taking it in with one glance, a gigantic wave of empathy swept over me that was not only for Seana, but for myself, too. *I had believed all that.* Though I tried so hard to rise, I had lived down to those ideas, and it had been like drinking poison.

Grabbing the poster down from the wall, I carried it with one hand through her downstairs studio and took the basement steps two at a time.

At the top of the stairs, I found her in our kitchen. It was evening now, and she was kneeling down on the dark brown hardwood floor in front of the stove, gently petting our Saint Bernard, Chloe. Love was literally oozing out of her and in that moment before she looked up, along with her stunning beauty I could see the deep sorrow and tremendous wound that had opened up. I caused that. *Shame on me.*

As soon as she saw me standing there, along with my expression of intense remorse, she must also have seen what was in my hands. The poster was ripped into several pieces. Taking it all in with one glance, Seana burst into tears and leapt up, throwing her arms around me in the rawest expression of deliverance and relief that I have ever had the honor of witnessing.

In one movement, we crumpled onto the floor—our arms, legs, and Chloe too—all tangled together. Hugging her tightly, I began to kiss her face and touch that wet, golden skin with my fingers in wonder and awe. Like a pilgrim blissfully lost, I traced long, whimsical trails with kisses that wound about and backtracked upon themselves. In her eyes, those two perfect windows of stormy blue sea, I saw reflected the utter exhaustion that stood isolated and alone at the core of her being. My wife, my Mooch, my beloved, had been at the end of herself, on the brink, and it crushed my heart as nothing else could have.

"Amore mio, amore mio. I am *so* sorry. I love you so much. I will *never* leave you. *Ever.* I will never ever leave you. I choose us. *I choose us.*"

There on the kitchen floor amid Chloe's absolute delight and her rolls of fur, sharing tears and laughter and holding tightly to my wife, into my mind's eye came our central wedding vow.

Slipping in unnoticed, as do so many things of great value, it is the thread upon which the other six vows were strung like iridescent pearls. They're the words I remember that my Baba once said to a couple preparing to marry. For our wedding, we had claimed them as our own, and I spoke them to her now.

"As long as there is breath left in me, we shall stay together, and I shall look upon you as Divine."

DAY ELEVEN

21. The Mokes

THE MOKULUA ISLANDS, or "the Mokes," as they're called by local *kama'āina*, are twin volcanic cones about a mile out from the Kailua coastline on the windward side of Oahu. When I first met Seana and tried to distract her with my increasingly complex lineup of fabulous island tourist experiences, the two islets were at the top of my list of places she had to visit before leaving Hawaii. That day was when *before Seana* and *after Seana* became a marker and a milestone, and over time, one of her favorite taglines.

Before Seana, the small stretch of sand on the northern Moke was the midpoint of my paddle—a place to rest, pivot, and return again. But it was also much more, and that was the main reason why I suggested it to her that day. Of all the vibrant, colorful visuals on the island, this one was by far my favorite. When I initially made the discovery ten years earlier, my admiration for the unmatched beauty that is Hawaii grew a thousandfold.

There is something magical about looking back upon Oahu that gives one true context. To see her whole, in one glance, is unlike any other island experience, and something that can only be truly appreciated from a distance.

I can imagine the moment when the ancient Polynesians first discovered Hawaii and their awe as they glimpsed the spectacle of this rare geographic anomaly. It's a chain of eight interconnected islands flung like diamonds on blue velvet, alone and adrift in the middle of the largest ocean on the planet. That must be why the modern Hawaiians, when they recreated the double-hulled voyaging canoes of their ancestors, named their first one, *Hōkūle'a* (*Star of Gladness*). For to turn and look back upon the islands is almost a revelation. Like nothing else, it puts into fresh perspective the history of the Earth and our place in it.

Two years to the June full moon *after Seana*, barefoot and newly wedded, we stepped directly from our Lanikai Beach ceremony into a Hawaiian outrigger canoe. It was decorated with *ti* leaves by dear friends who paddled us out to the sand at Moku Nui, the big Moke, while family and friends watched from Lanikai Beach. From their perspective, once we had passed beyond the reef, we were just two more grains of white and beige in the sand. Meanwhile, Seana and I wandered alone on that little beach, spellbound.

Over the years, each time we returned to Hawaii, Seana requested that we go down before dawn to our wedding spot at the far end of Lanikai Beach and renew our vows. Then, she would paddle her longboard out about a third of the way to the Mokes as the sun was just starting to climb between the twin cones, sit up, and stretch out her arms toward the horizon. The visual was stunning.

Etched into my memory is Seana amid a painter's palette of living color—glittering hues of purple, cerulean blue, dark chocolate, aquamarine, burnt orange—and down the middle, an oscillating, golden path of sunlight that bisects the sphere. Centered within it all is Seana on her board. She is a speck on the vast ocean, arms wide open to the rising sun, sea, sky, and beyond.

WITH JUST TWO days left, there were a fair number of things to do. The only problem was that most of them required forethought and premeditated action, two things that for the last week and a half were at odds with my condition. What I craved were their antipoles, the opposites of all they represented. The closer I drew to the thirteenth day, the stronger my longing for the healing touch of silence and nature with a liberal amount of meditation and chanting sprinkled in. For like nothing else, the practices had become my anchor in the storm.

It was a real dilemma, this so-called healing. Eleven days earlier there had been a complete system reboot, and I knew it was only a matter of time before my brain completed its rewiring of before and after Seana. Whereas she had always loved the idea of there being a *before and after Seana*, where life was better together because we were together, this *after Seana* was not what either of us had ever imagined.

But the neurons in my brain were only trying to be helpful, doing what six million years of evolution designed them to do—normalize something that was not remotely normal. Strange as it sounds, it was as if I'd struck oil. Rich and fleeting, I knew the rare gifts that had been flowing up and out through the opening could stop at any moment. These were ephemeral. They were like her, morning dewdrops on a blade of grass. My chief concern was that it might become like the dream you know holds an immensely important message, only to have it vanish within a few seconds of waking. To me, the possibility of that seemed calamitous and almost on a par with losing her.

So much appeared different from even yesterday, but actually, little had changed besides geography. I now had a growing sense that this process would not be wrapping up after just two more days either. Where such blind optimism had sprung from, I know not. The loving devastation kept coming, sped up by a mysterious force and cycling through me like seasons gone haywire.

So, I set up calls with my principal and superintendent on Vashon to request more time off, arranged a video chat with my fifth graders for next week, and got on social media to leave one more message for the online ohana. Then, I intended to fully surrender myself to the healing *mana* of Hawaii—that divine spirit that coexists in every molecule of its mountains, sea, and people.

One unexpected bonus of getting online was seeing that Seana's mother, Jana, appeared to be well-supported and responding positively. Abundant expressions of love followed all of her posts like the wake from a huge ocean liner. In fact, Aunt Shelley, Uncle Gary, and the entire Lowe family seemed to be handling it far better than I could have hoped, and everyone in that part of the Midwest looked to be slowly emerging from the storm, brought together as they were by the tragedy, even as it had torn them apart.

It was also obvious that word of Seana's thirteenth day had grown tenfold. Not only were heavenly, heart-wrenching tributes continuing to stream in, but they were being shared and commented on by scores of people I didn't even know. Not surprisingly, the inner group of Seana's friends, which of course included the three who had accompanied me to the mortuary, were all leaving beautiful, heartrending testimonials. But one of the most remarkable side effects of this whole thing was learning about people whom Seana had only referenced from her past.

Names that for so many years I'd only heard about began to materialize on social media, and it was clear they felt summoned. Although I knew almost nothing about them or their connection to Seana, reading their online tributes told me everything.

At last I understood why so-and-so had to be called every month or visited on Seana's way to Detroit or Senegal. In their expressions of immense loss and gratitude, faceless souls stood naked and visible for the first time. Each one was holding a common thread that bound us all together—utter amazement that such a one as her had walked among us before winking and blinking out like a shooting star on a cloudy night.

Even people I knew quite well showed up differently, metamorphosing into someone I'd never really seen before, or at least not fully. Of course, Seana had always known who they were, even if sometimes they themselves didn't, which is why they loved her so completely.

To give an idea of the beauty that was revealing itself online, though too numerous to include more, here is one such tribute from a friend and colleague.

> Ageless, timeless, effervescent, wide-awake Seana.
> Unceasingly optimistic, consonant, fierce with
> loving clarity. Authentic, present, in gratitude, and
> always, always cultivating and seizing the nectar
> of life. The sun was always shining when you were
> around. This is how I know you, Seana.

You walked the walk like no one I've ever met. Your one thousand percent dedication and ardent sincerity extended to me, your Amore Barron, friends, family, colleagues, your work, the planet— everything you touched. A true Taoist, you embodied naturalness, ease, and spontaneity. You could also kick some serious ass.

You were my (and everyone's) tireless cheerleader. It was simply in your generous nature to advocate. You were on a personal mission to be an instrument for our highest actualization. I don't know how many dozens of my silk marma masks you got for your tribe, how many bottles of organic skin care, how many down pillows and duvet covers, all the while thanking me for making beauty in the world.

I remember when you received adverse health diagnoses, fingers and toes numb, organs compromising your forward momentum. You, in all your aliveness, refused to wear that mantle, resolutely committing yourself to an even higher level of health and self-care. Girl, you fucking rocked it and healed yourself and kept going, beaming that magnificent smile at everyone lucky enough to be nearby.

I remember fifteen or so years ago when you were remodeling your Longmont home. We were remodeling ours too and you enthusiastically upcycled our 1950s toilet and tub. Only you, Seana! That was your commitment to the planet in action.

To describe you, Seana, as universally beloved is a gross understatement. But it is only a reflection of how you gave of yourself, selflessly, tirelessly.

No matter where each of us was on the planet,
you made a point to not only be in contact (our
monthly "dates") but to have meaningful connection. I've never known a person more dedicated
to SHOWING UP. You must have known what
an inspiration you were to so many people, who
you touched deeply in ways no one else could,
and whose life trajectories you change simply by
BEING YOU. That must have felt so good. Your
light and love were contagious.

Beyond my own selfish grief, I mourn the
world's loss, because if any one person was spark-
ing transformation in a million hearts, it was you,
beloved Seana. Fierce, unapologetic, and unstoppable is how I feel and see you. And I know you
would have wanted only goodness to come from
this—I'm saying it—fucking devastating tragedy.
In the past thirteen days I have felt your inordinate
strength, your compassion and your perseverance,
among a thousand other positive qualities, stirring
in me. Your life was your message. As one of your
friends eloquently said, "I will be the Seana I want
to see in the world."

This story does not end here. I feel and see you
all around me. These words only scratch the surface.
I am keeping our monthly dates and I know I am
not alone when I say I still hear your words and will,
in my own way, carry your spirit's message forward.
Love was your legacy and in that I WILL NOT LET
YOU DOWN, SEANA.

You are here and will always be. But I will surely

miss the hell out of the embodiment of your soul's grace. Onward, Seana. Onward.

Forty-eight hours from liftoff, across the globe from San Francisco to West Africa, pods of colleagues, past students, family, and friends were all coordinating plans to meet up. It was an online web of interconnection unlike any I had ever imagined. But wherever you were in the world on that day, you could share in the sacred act of sending Seana into the light.

And although I did not accept any of the invitations to join in, nor publicize my private plans, they had at last become clear to me. At sunrise, I would be on the beach where we first met and were married, encircled by her other muse, nature. Then, facing the Mokes, I would chant the song of power and Oneness, the Guru Gita—and along with a coconut, flowers, and a jar of her ashes, offer them all to the sea.

As Swamiji had outlined that I might, this final flurry of activity also consisted of writing and posting a letter of thanks and praise to my beloved as a model to others who were still seeking guidance on how to offer her blessings on the thirteenth day. The post included what felt like the perfect quote from one of her favorite films, *Shakespeare in Love,* and closed with a coda of profound love and respect.

Philip Henslowe: Mr. Fennyman, allow me to explain about the theatre business. The natural condition is one of insurmountable obstacles on the road to imminent disaster.

Hugh Fennyman: So what do we do?

Philip Henslowe: Nothing. Strangely enough, it all turns out well.

Hugh Fennyman: How?

Philip Henslowe: I don't know. It's a mystery.

Amore, I will always be a "Yes" to the mystery with you. Now SOAR, my Beloved.

Sharing something so deeply personal was somehow strangely liberating. It felt fearless, and like it might set her into motion one day early. After reading through several times, its keen sense of intimacy eventually called up the Pablo Neruda poem that Seana had once used as *her* coda to me in one of our earliest communications. For some time afterwards I was lost, disappearing and reappearing within the light-filled reverie of what happens whenever we join together.

> "I love you in this way because I know no other way
> of loving but this, in which there is no I or you, so
> intimate that your hand upon my chest is my hand,
> so intimate that when I fall asleep it is your eyes
> that close." —Pablo Neruda

AROUND THE SIX-month mark after Seana and I first met, I began to realize that, although one may fly high on delirious virtual conversations for a long time, for those in love video chats can sometimes evolve into glorious acts of futility.

Seana had returned home to Colorado, and we were in daily correspondence. But as yet we had no specific plans to bridge the ocean between us, even if each day it seemed increasingly likely that we would. Still, how does one know when to commit to a change so consequential? Ultimately, it was the ocean itself that told me to leave Hawaii.

Outer Pua'ena Point on the North Shore of Oahu is an excellent example of a reef that is open to powerful winter swells, except that it's even more potent than some of the other surf spots in Hawaii because its waves break below sea level. Ironically, just around the corner, inner Pua'ena Point is the perfect beginner's surf spot and a place where many tourists, including Seana, learned to surf within its protected bay.

However, when the swell becomes extra-large, the outside point just to the north comes alive. Because of the unique nature of the reef and its bathymetry, you can't see the bottom of the wave from a distance. This means that the largest ones come in low, hugging the ocean floor, and remain almost invisible until suddenly cresting. Then, all at once, they hit the reef. If you're out of position even by a few yards, you won't see them until they're almost on top of you.

One afternoon when my Aikahi fifth graders had all left for the day, I heard the surf was on the rise and headed up to the North Shore. When I finally arrived at Pua'ena, the sun was already low on the horizon so I did not take the time to watch it before going out. Any experienced surfer will tell you this is really, really stupid—especially on a rapidly rising swell in the mid-Pacific.

Although I'd surfed some large waves in Hawaii, a big swell at Pua'ena's outer reef is a combination lock of dangers that must be solved each and every time you enter the water. In addition to breaking below sea level, the outer point's shoreline is really not a beach at all but a solid, unbroken lava wall that extends the length of the outer point, sharp as razors and completely impass-able from any direction. To even graze it lightly is to cut yourself bloody.

The only way to get in or out is to paddle around the point from the inner bay where the surf is much smaller and the beach has some sand. In fact, the inner shoreline of that outer reef is akin to a death zone, because after large swells break, the white-water sweeps across the lava beds in only two inches of water with no escape route.

Out in the water that afternoon, there were quite a few of us, and I was finding it really difficult to get a wave to myself. After about half an hour, the sun had begun to set over the water, and a medium-sized wave rolled through. I paddled hard, but just missed catching it.

Huge mistake.

Now I was caught too far inside, and as soon as I swung my board around I could see the long, horizontal lines of a much larger set drawing on the reef.

Unlike anything I've ever known, the fear of drowning reaches into the deepest parts of the muscles and brain. Once felt, the body never forgets. Looking out at the massive set, somatic fear and adrenaline shot into my bloodstream as if they'd been injected intravenously. Even digging into the water as hard and as fast as I could, I barely slipped under the first wave of the set. As soon as I came up, I looked out to sea and shuddered at the sight of the next one.

Fully hitting the sunken reef, it was going to break a lot farther outside than any wave that afternoon. I stroked furiously, but I knew that there was no way to cover the distance. With only a slim chance of slipping fully beneath it, as the wave was launch-ing forward I tried to sneak under the lip. But even though I was partially submerged, it landed just close enough to the back of my board that it stole all the momentum I would need to break through the back of the wave. Without that thrust, it sucked me backwards over the falls on my board and into the impact zone.

The whiteout of the impact zone is where the waves break. It's where you don't want to be on a large day of surf and something you really want to avoid if there are multiple waves in the set. But it is especially where you never want to be on a big day at outer Pua'ena Point. This is because in large to extra-large Hawaiian surf, another of the many hazards of this particular spot is that at lower tides it has a fully exposed lava rock sitting directly in the middle of the white, foamy impact zone.

About two car lengths long and a car length wide, the huge mass of dried lava sits there jutting out of the water like a small island. The entire surface is crisscrossed by thousands of lava holes and miniature tunnels, and it's the one landmark that every local knows to avoid at all costs.

When I came up from the beating of the last wave, I found that I had been spun around and was now facing the shore. There, directly in front of me not two yards away and blocking my line of sight to the shoreline, was the lava rock. It sat there foaming white-water through its chutes and tiny crevices like a living, breathing demon of the sea. As soon as I saw the rock, I recognized that I was in serious danger, and I became absolutely terrified. Worst of all, I had a strong feeling that there was another wave coming up behind me in the set.

When I turned around to look back out to sea and first saw it, I understood perfectly that this situation was far beyond me, and my mind briefly went blank. Then, the thoughts went berserk, shouting commands to my arms to dig deep and legs to kick with everything they had left.

In surfing, anything of importance often happens within seconds, and there is simply no time to stop and think things through rationally. You rely completely on your physical strength, ocean knowledge, and all the years of prior experience. That's part of what makes surfing so compelling. It's wildly unpredictable, and can be life-threatening even on a small day.

I could see that the wave now standing up on the reef was going to break in front of me. There would be no chance whatsoever of slipping even partially underneath. Nor could I turn and paddle back toward shore or laterally because of the huge boulder behind me. I was in the worst-case scenario. As a surfer, the possibility of this predicament will keep you up at night and completely out of the water at others. When you're caught inside, as I clearly was about to be, it means that the weight and power of the wave is going to explode either on you or very near.

A familiar verb used for a crashing wave in hollow, large surf is that *it detonates.* The other verb that often accompanies it in a sentence is *annihilate.* As in, *I got annihilated.* These are appropriate because when a big wave explodes directly in front of you, there's no telling what will happen. It can break your board in half, cause severe injury, or worse. Of course, I knew all of this without having to think, but my paramount concern was the lava rock directly behind me. I had to get as far away from it as possible before the wave broke.

The dilemma was that every stroke away from the boulder would take me closer to the mountain of moving water. Normally, if you're caught inside, you can paddle in toward shore to avoid taking the full brunt of a wave's power. The farther you are from the point where the heaving lip meets the water, the less intense the impact is likely to be. Even a few yards can make a huge difference. But in this case, the boulder blocked this possibility, so I was in a quandary.

Nonetheless, of the two—the wave or the rock—the small island of lava was by far the greater risk. Intuitively, I understood that my best odds were to try to position myself as equidistant as possible from both of them just as it landed. I would need to time my duck dive perfectly. I'd still get annihilated, but at least I would have a chance. The timing was positively critical. If I submerged too early, I would already be popping up like a cork just as the wave unloaded.

As soon as I was a few yards from where the lip was going to hit, I began to push the front of my board downward with great force. Before going under, in what felt like slow motion, I glanced up one last time at what was about to unleash itself and was shocked to see that it looked considerably worse than I had previously thought. The wave had turned out to be much bigger once its energy engaged the reef.

Spontaneously from deep inside, all at once inside my head I heard my own inner voice yelling loudly, filling the entire space of mental awareness.

GURUMAYI, I NEED YOU NOW!

Now, it's not like I regularly call out to her for help. In fact, in twenty-five years this was the first time I had ever uttered those words or anything like them. To hear myself shouting them inside my head as I was submerging underwater actually startled me, and instinctively I knew that my body understood itself to be in imminent danger.

With that, everything exploded at once, ripping the board from my arms like a stuffed toy from a child. Violent and deep, it pushed me downward, thrashing me in several directions. Then, just as suddenly, I was lifted up and launched backwards in the direction of the shoreline. I curled into a ball, covered my head, and waited for it—the crunch of bones against lava. Weightless, I even had time to wonder how I was going to get away from the knives of the inner lava beds once the ocean surge carried me in.

But it never came. Instead of being crushed against the lava rock, I suddenly found myself lying on top of it. I don't even remember landing, except that it was gentle, like I was placed there by a giant hand. Utterly amazed, I realized that the explosion must have thrown me so high up that I missed the front edge of the little island and had come to rest on top. Just as inexplicably, I had somehow touched down with my board partially under me.

After a large wave breaks, water levels surge and swirl for a few seconds in between pulsations. It's almost as if the ocean is exhausted, trying to catch its breath, and breathing hard. Especially around exposed rocks and reef, the mean sea level will often rise and fall a few feet or more in the wake of a large swell. So, as soon as the first backwash began its surge up and over the top of the boulder, in one swift movement, I leapt off the front edge of the rock with my board back into the ocean.

Feverish and in a total panic, I paddled parallel to shore and to my left, away from the impact zone and in the direction of the small inner bay at Pua'ena.

After about ten strokes, two things became crystal clear. First, my arms had no strength left to paddle. I could not even raise my elbows completely out of the water. And second, there was no next wave. The set was over. I had time. I was going to make it to the inner bay.

With the shot of adrenaline fully spent, my body felt depleted in a way I had never before experienced. My mind was as translucent as a cloudless sky on the clearest night of the year. When at last a thought materialized, I was just entering the safe zone of the inner bay so that my intellect had the benefit of the long silence preceding it for extra contrast.

The thought-message sprung forth unconsciously, and just like the one before the wave detonated, it was unequivocal and direct. Actually, it sounded like a command.

You fucking idiot. Go be with Seana.

Few messages in my life have ever been more clear. Shortly thereafter, the relatives came out to share their opinions as well, although they were more critical of me.

What the hell are you doing out in surf this large? And on a rising swell! You are truly, truly stupid. These waves are WAY too big.

You idiot! Go be with Seana.

Needless to say, this became one of her favorite stories. In future years, each time we visited Hawaii, Seana and I would stay a week on the North Shore and always spend at least one or two sunny afternoons surfing and relaxing at the small sandy beach of inner Pua'ena Point. Then, we'd take a short walk up around the outer point and pay homage to the small island of black lava that, of course, Seana dubbed "our rock."

Day Twelve

22. Shaktipat

I HAVE BEEN to all the places I know you'd go. Do you know that I am looking for you? I've seen such beauty. Lanikai colors in turquoise and gold. But the form that I love is not there.

Of course, I know better than to expect to see you, meet you, talk to you. I touched your body a few days ago—the cold, stiff vehicle that you left behind. It filled me with joy to honor you in this way, to wave a flame around your vacant face, to place a picture of you right next to it to remind me which is which. In it, you were radiant, filled with your unique light. But still, I had to thank your body in person. What service it gave to you, to me, and to the world around us. It was healing to touch your skin with sacred ash. It felt perfect that day, just like the mantras at the end of the morning chant, "This is perfect. That is perfect ..."

But today is not that day. I am sitting in a car parked in my friend's yard crying, missing you, wondering where you are and why we can't talk together anymore. Why haven't you spoken to me in so long other than through my pen?

What a mystery, the unknown. Everything, including you, my dear one, comes out of it and then dissolves back into it. But where are you in that? What are you doing? What are you learning? I want to learn too. We always shared everything. Remember radical honesty? The free fall? That's how we started this whole journey together. Such commitment! All in!

Amore mio, you always were and still are nothing but a flame of love. But I love the form you took this time around. I will always love the form you took.

THE LAST THING on my to-do list before the thirteenth day is to sign up again for the Intensive, and a second offering is quickly approaching. Sharing about Siddha Yoga or the Shaktipat Intensive has never been easy for me, and I'm careful about sounding overzealous. But I guess in one sense you could say that I have never done a better job of getting the word out. I remember someone once saying to me, "If someone asks for a glass of water, don't hose him down," and so I share with the online ohana a very brief recommendation along with the upcoming date and link.

The idea of retaking the Intensive is concurrently intriguing and genuinely agitating. The reasons seem obvious, but perhaps it is also because I recently learned from the autopsy that the timing of Seana's accident and subsequent cardiac arrest in the emergency room all took place squarely within the Intensive's first session. In fact, her time of death was the exact same time *to the minute* that the morning meditation session ended.

SHAKTIPAT IS A rare and priceless gift that can be utterly life-transforming and sometimes dangerous. Initially, it can also feel as if nothing much has happened. If you ever find yourself in the presence of the rare master who can bestow it, just know that, somewhere deep inside, you have made a profound decision.

In one sense, this highly impactful choice means that you'd had enough. Fed up with endless patterns of chasing dreams, only to discover again and again that no matter what breathtaking, favorable event or individual at long last has appeared in your life—it or he or she or you, always disappears.

And so to pursue an extraordinary number of promising-looking streams that each end up spilling out in a tangled confluence of rapture, suffering, and sorrow is a painful but often compulsory way to learn what I have come to think of as *the* life lesson: let go. At least it is surely one of my principal lessons this lifetime, and it has been brought to my attention that, before I leave this body, it is of paramount importance that I learn to unhitch from my need to control. We have no control over anything. We never did.

Hypnotized by our maze-like efforts and desires, we simply haven't been paying close enough attention to the repeating cycles that come and go in endless pulsation—pleasure and pain, acquiring and losing, light and shadow. In the pandemonium of all that exertion, a honed selfishness spreads unseen like a horrible disease. Consequently, we miss out on the beauty and light that was, and is, already present—even as it is passing us by on its way back to the formless source from whence it came.

Nevertheless, it would be wise to understand beforehand that shaktipat, the igniting of the dormant Kundalini energy within us through grace, can also mean the arrival of radical change. And while it marks a turning point on the spiritual journey that is precious beyond all other earthly gifts, it necessarily will have its counterpoint in the eventual remodeling of one's outer world to match the inner revolution.

Accordingly, it carries the distinct possibility that over time everything you have worked so hard to amass, align, and bring under control in your life will be spiraling out and away before too long, like the trails of visible light from galaxies that died millions of years ago.

Since shaktipat, the infusion of energy from a spiritual master, is said to eventually lead to liberation, it begs the question of liberation from what? Anything that stands in the way of its goal of transcendent love and growth, which ends up being pretty much everything.

> *Shaktipat: (lit. the descent of grace) The transmission of spiritual power (shakti) from the guru to the student; spiritual awakening by grace.*

OF ALL THE extraordinary things that my wondrous, coloratura, complex mother contributed to my life, there is one incomparable gift for which I will never be able to fully express the extent of my gratitude. In fact, without it, I am quite certain that I would never have met Seana, for I would not have been ready for her.

When I was twenty years old, one day my mother came to me, my two older sisters, and grandpa and said, "Today, I'm going to take you all to meet a real holy man." It was 1981, and just down the street from where we lived in Santa Monica Canyon a huge white tent had been erected next to the beach.

We all piled into the station wagon and headed down to the boardwalk. Approaching the tent, I made out a dark man in flowing orange clothes in the distance walking swiftly across the parking lot. It would have been difficult not to notice him because he was being followed by a growing crowd, and everyone around me stopped whatever they were doing to watch him.

My mother said that his name was Swami Muktananda, a meditation master from India, and affectionately known as Baba. A few years earlier in Oakland, she had taken something called a Shaktipat Intensive with him, and even though she was a lifelong Catholic, that experience was apparently how she knew that he was a real holy man.

Inside the tent and starting that very day, Baba was launching a three-day chant. I had no idea what an Indian chant was or might be like, but there were thousands of people gathering for it, and an electric atmosphere pervaded the immense, make-shift pavilion.

Hung from one wall of the tent was a blue neon sign, OM NAMAH SHIVAYA. I learned that it was the mantra of their lineage, meaning "I honor my inner Self," and one of the primary methods a Siddha guru bestows shaktipat. Those three words, Om Namah Shivaya, would turn out to be the only words of the chant for the next three days and nights.

Just before the chant began, Baba's only instruction that I remember was, "Don't fall asleep." My family stayed for an hour or two, yet I was just beginning to settle in and becoming more and more determined to dive into the experience as deeply as possible.

At one point later in the evening, I had the thought, *How cool would it be to try and chant for three days in a row!* And so began my long hours and late nights, shuttling between my home and the tent.

Across the arc of those days and nights, I recall bright flashes as if in time-lapse: the sweet, exotic smell of burning incense; the lead chanters and musicians at the front of the hall changing places like dancers in near-perfect sync; bodies swaying for hours

in the dark as if pulled to and fro by an enormous, invisible counterweight from somewhere high above.

More than anything else, I remember the droning of the
Indian musical instruments in combination with the syllables of
the mantra, especially late at night when it sounded like we were
all intoxicated and the tent seemed to lean sideways in empathy
with our bodies and the pitch of our voices. Apparently, the syllables of the mantra could be stretched like caramel and taste like
it too, for it inhabited my mind in elongated swaths of silence
where no thoughts or words interrupted. No matter. No description could have described it accurately anyway.

When at last the chant came to an end on the final morning,
the tent was filled to capacity. Baba gave a short talk, sat back
in his chair onstage, and a young Brahmin priest came out and
recited some extremely complex Sanskrit mantras. After a little
while, my mind began to wander, and I remember thinking, *This
was really interesting. I wonder who is down at the beach today?*

As soon as I had this thought, the priest began to forget the
words. Like an impending train wreck, this had the immediate
effect of yanking me out of my daydream. Stopping and starting, the young man kept trying to regain the flow but could not
remember the exact sequence. Several times he would recall some
piece of it, only to falter once again. Finally, he stopped altogether,
unable to continue.

In the ensuing silence, I'll never forget my image of him. His
head was bowed forward, chin to white shirt, and the look of melancholy on his young face was heartbreaking.

Suddenly, from about ten yards behind him onstage, Baba
leaned forward in his chair and began to tell him the forgotten
mantras. Soon, the young priest caught the sequence, and in that
moment three things happened simultaneously.

First, Baba leaned back into his chair. Second, something about Baba's movements and expression absolutely froze me. They were completely free of judgment and empty of any self-interest, whatsoever. I'd never seen anything remotely like it, and it struck me in the same way as if he'd picked up a large rock and thrown it at my head. Instantly, I burst out crying with a huge sob that leapt out from the center of my chest and heart, crushing them both inward.

And third, as soon as I cried out, Baba whipped his head and stared directly into my eyes.

In surprise and shock, I hid my face from him behind the others around me while continuing to weep uncontrollably. A few seconds later I looked up and he was still staring right at me. Dumbfounded, I hid myself once again, wondering, *How does he know?*

At that point, the young Brahmin faltered again. I glanced up only to see Baba leaning forward and feeding him the missing mantras, but as soon as I looked, Baba turned his head to look at me *while still speaking the mantras.* Once more I hid, but each time I looked up he was either already staring at me or would turn to stare at me in the same instant. It was as if he knew exactly when to look.

Finally, the Brahmin no longer needed his help, and when last I glanced up, Baba was not looking. He never looked at me again. Ever.

Sitting near the back of the tent and to the left, amid a crowd of some three thousand people, I sat there baffled and in shock.

How had he known? What can it possibly mean?

A few minutes later, the event ended with *darshan,* an Indian tradition where people can come forward to bow with respect, receiving in turn the sage's blessings and grace. I waited for almost an hour in the long, winding line. Along the way I recalled my mother's story of how, just like this, she had approached him a few years ago after an Intensive. Whereas for others he had sprinkled but a few drops of holy water onto their heads, when she bowed before him he dumped the entire vessel.

So as I got closer, I found myself expecting him at the very least to pull me aside and acknowledge what had occurred between us. Instead, his work already done, Baba paid me no attention whatsoever, bopping me on the head with his peacock wand without even looking at me.

Soon after, I left the tent, not to return. But a seed was planted and a flame lit. Two months later, Baba and the tent left the boardwalk and the United States. A little more than one year later, his physical form would leave us all, as well.

I AM SITTING on our spot in the sand at the far end of Lanikai Beach just a few feet from the ocean's edge. Like a line of demarcation, the horizon perfectly divides the sea and sky. Out there the limitless blue sea feels solidly real, and the sky too, but not quite as much.

Above that impeccable line are clouds and the Earth's atmosphere, but then nothing but an infinity of planets and stars and the unknown, and so it becomes something abstract and imaginary to me. There is no end to what I don't know.

"What we know of life is only where we have decided to rest with our questioning." That Fran Peavey quote was one that I heard Seana use on many occasions to guide and encourage her students to go deeper into social issues and especially personal reflections. So often, in fact, that it became one of my all-time favorites to use with my own students, child and adult alike.

Tomorrow will surely bring another line of demarcation, yet another iteration of *before and after Seana*. There have been so many of these already that metaphors such as "the layers of an onion" or "why temples have a sanctum sanctorum" have begun to feel more like factual descriptions than the simpler explanation: "Your wife is dead, and it will take time."

What will take time? You mean the pain will heal and the love will fade? You mean I will no longer feel ripped open like a ripe fruit, and all this will end? You just cannot know how many rooms you'll have to enter and depart to get to the innermost sanctuary of the temple if you've never been inside it before.

The very first photo I took of Seana sits propped up in the sand against the small jar of her ashes that I brought from Colorado. On my towel beside it is a coconut and a copy of the Colorado State Trooper's Accident Report that I downloaded and have now read through, diagrams and all. Things are getting pretty surreal down at the beach.

Yet here and now, nature is my anchor and is doing all it can for me. Effortlessly, of course, for that is the nature of nature. Fully engaging all my senses at once with its humility and limitless beauty, it's a perfect reminder that I am still in a body, even if she is not.

Nature was always her muse. Even during work deadlines, Seana would schedule a solitary walk through the forest or a horseback ride. It was genuinely puzzling at times and frustrating at others, because later I might see her unsatisfied with the quality of her submitted work. But, of course, she knew. The power of connecting to something greater than ourselves inevitably brings out our best, regardless of how it may appear.

The sun has been steadily climbing above the Mokuluas, and when the clouds finally part, a blinding path of light along the surface of the water comes directly for me. Overexposed, the little Moke (Moku Iki) stands like a fuzzy, dark pyramid as the only identifiable object within that brilliance.

But for Seana in the center of the photograph, the outer scene is an exact replica of the one at the foot of the towel. It's stunning in its contrast, like she's been superimposed into the frame. In the seed photo, she stands at the water's edge between these same two islets, water lapping against her feet, smiling blithely and oblivious to what's awaiting her.

Moving my eyes back and forth several times from the photo to the actual is a child's game and, predictably, a mesmerizing one. The ineffable sweetness of her presence defies time and space, perpetuating the illusion. Knowing that in that moment she does not know what's coming nor how much we will alter each other, we have come full circle.

As such, along with the warmth of the sand and sun, Swamiji's words seem to have seeped into everything around me.

"Have you ever read the *Yoga Vasistha*? I mean your journey reminds me of it. You know, how someone goes into a dream, lives for a whole lifetime, and they wake up a moment later in the same place …. And it's like you think it's some fantasy, but we each go through these journeys which don't leave any traces, in some ways like the ocean. They come, they are very real, and then we move on. And this is what at the end is called our life's journey, and who could have imagined it? It's dreamlike and very real at the same time. I keep seeing us there on the beach. Your journey happens from there, and you come back with this amazing vision. Who would know what joy, what pain, would be waiting for you?"

Oddly, or perhaps naturally, this epiphany politely escorts me back into the present moment, such that *here and now* completes its merging with *there and then*. And with this inner shift, the last line from the poem that I most associate with Seana leaps up and then settles down into my mind and heart like Mary Oliver's grasshopper flinging herself from the grass.

"Tell me, what is it you plan to do with your one wild and precious life?"

It opens the gates wide, of course, for that verse *is* my wife. She embodied it. Not only for herself, but apparently for many others too, because it is a recurring theme running through her online tributes like a river running through mountains and across foothills to the sea. Without our even knowing, she interconnects us all.

"The Summer Day" is a poem that will wake you up if you let it. Its life-giving waters pour through me now in the form of gratitude and unspoken longing and the great goodness of being allowed to be lost in love. All this, and nothing to wipe my face and blow my nose with but my shirt.

Sometime later, the wave passes through, gently returning me across the shimmering turquoise sea to the sand. Floating in deep equipoise like the white, fluffy clouds in the blue sky overhead, I pick up my chanting book from the morning Guru Gita and look for the line within the verse at the end that has been jumping out at me for days in a row.

I do this as much from the feeling that it holds a great mystery as from my inability to comprehend it. But I like what it says very much, and I know she would too. I hope to understand, one day, that it may be possible.

"O beloved, you are My very Self forever."

Ironically, even though I was the one chanting all those years, Seana may have been the one to have the better understanding of that verse. Filled with contentment, I set the small book down.

And then I begin to release her.

DAY THIRTEEN

23. Onward

> Infinite blessings to name and celebrate ... I am
> grateful for the gift of my life every moment of
> every day and wish the same deep contentment of a
> fulfilled heart to all. ONWARD.
> —Dr. Seana Lowe Steffen, 50th birthday, August
> 28, 2017

A FEW MONTHS after we met, Seana returned to Hawaii a
second time. An exceptionally gifted instructor herself, one
day she came and sat in on my fifth-grade classroom.

At a book sale in the cafeteria later that afternoon, I came across
a small children's book written by Patrick McDonnell, *The Gift of
Nothing*. Nestled like a rare bird in between *Captain Underpants*
and *Star Wars*, I made a gift of it to her, and in time the story of
Mooch and Earl grew into a cherished part of ours as well.

Mooch (a cat) is looking for the perfect gift for her best friend,

Earl (a pooch). She wonders, *What do you get someone who has everything?*

It dawns on her. *Nothing!*

So, after looking everywhere for nothing and not finding it, she finally gets a really big empty box (because it was a *lot* of nothing).

When Earl opens it, he declares, "There's nothing here!"

"Yesh!" says Mooch. "Nothing ... but me and you!"

And so, arm in arm, and looking out a snowy window upon a vast sea of stars, Mooch and Earl just stay still, enjoying nothing—*and everything.*

THE WAVES ARE crashing farther outside on Lanikai Reef this morning with a singular sound that is somehow both arrhythmic and hypnotic. What beauty. I am forever grateful to Hawaii—to the *'āina, moana, aloha,* and especially her *mana.*

It's been thirteen days since I heard the officer's words, "She is deceased." I've returned to where we began, but I don't see her. She is not walking across my beach with a camera around her neck, nor is she in the sea seated on her surfboard, arms stretched open to the heavens. Not that she was supposed to be, and not like I need the proof, but I brought the photograph again to remind me of something. I am just not sure what. So, I replay it in my head.

"Aloha! I wonder, would you like me to use that massive camera to take your picture in front of the Mokuluas?"

That's how I got her to pause with me on this very spot twelve years ago. It was a smooth move, she said. We both laughed. Yet any lover will tell you the same. You have to find a way. How else do you stop the infinite long enough to see if it recognizes you?

And I guess this is what I want to talk about today—*the extraordinary mystery of the formless.* Having been through the fire, reduced to ashes, and lived to tell, I am no longer afraid to wonder aloud. Before Seana, it seemed like a stretch, a betrayal even, to imagine that a loved one's passing could somehow be a gift, a blessing equal to the sum of everything they are. But I feel fearless now. Which is not that big a deal, of course. After all, what else can be taken from me? What do I have left to lose? There is no one that I love like her.

So, here is what I am wondering.

Would not love unconditionally find a way to make even death be of benefit? Might not the lover's final exhale carry with it a wish and strong intention for great blessings and insight to befall the beloved? Not later, after the sordid details have already lain down in the grass, but right now. Let it start *now*. For is there ever a more truly fertile moment in life than death?

That beautiful one, whether she appears to disappear or vice versa, was a slingshot and a catapult—and most certainly a gift. Seana's final gift of love to me was her disappearance. I have put all my efforts into staying open to the blessings that continually emanate from that pure offering. How perfect that her final written chapter in the book, *Innovation in Environmental Leadership*, begins, "From Peril to Possibility ..." for this is how Seana approached everything in life. She was always the first to ask—what is possible, and how can we turn this breakdown into a breakthrough?

Nevertheless, I am also aware that I will never fully recover. Unable to see and hear her stunning, rarest of the rare, golden form, follows me daily like my shadow. And perhaps that is as it must be for growth to continue freely and abundantly. Maybe this awareness that I will not be recovering ever is a sign of radically good health, and not a wound to be borne dutifully.

I found that I have a choice. The power of that choice has

revealed every shard as love, every heart-wrenching moment of missing her beautiful, never-to-be-seen-again form as love. Remembering her divine virtues creates fresh tears in garlands of gratitude. I feel an upwelling of love and a heart breaking open for the perfection and beauty of our shared existence, and a subtle desire to somehow benefit others from what I am learning.

I think it is a gift of acceptance—this surrender to what is and must be—that I can continue onward and rebuild an entire life without her. It is an awesome undertaking. Even now, it appears to be an impossible task. To imagine my life without her by my side guiding our choices and reveling in our shared delight at the grandness of this one wild and precious life, this is new. But I get *appearance* now. It is the stage on which we play.

Because of this, I am able to drink the elixir of my wife's final gift fully, and I have come to realize that I never have to stop drinking in the insights, the expansion, and the love.

Strewn among the magnificent field of divine virtues that I witnessed in her presence, two are nectar. And so, using Seana's own words, "I choose love and acceptance."

Such gifts and insights into my purpose for being alive keep me company now. After all, I, too, am here for only a little while before I crash back into the sea one last time. So, I thank you, my Muse and my teachers, with a full heart for the gift of these days and nights—the time and space to surrender and learn, to cry out and to grow—and to learn to love very, very well.

EPILOGUE

WHETHER OR NOT you knew Seana matters little. Don't let that stop you. She always befriended quickly and easily, anyway. And so, in my mind I'm imagining that you are speaking to her three nights before she will disappear unannounced. You're asking her the same question that she asked me in that moment.

"What one thing would you want me to remember tonight before I go to sleep?"

And she says to you, "I would want you to remember your purpose for being alive."

Because it is possible that Seana asked me that question not just for her benefit, but for ours too. If there is one thing I continue to learn, it's that goodness can see very far. Past and future are like playthings to the vision of the present moment.

So, if she were here and now (and perhaps she is, peering over your shoulder and reading these words right along with you—or even more delicious to consider, she is reading them *through* your eyes), it seems to me that the final gift of her disappearance was also intended for you—that you, and she, are calling to you. The beloved has been here before, and will come again. Why not in you, as you?

May you remember your purpose for being alive.
Don't fall asleep.
Onward.
Don't fall back asleep.

ACKNOWLEDGMENTS

THIS IS IN profound acknowledgment of the lineage of teachers of Siddha Yoga: Gurumayi, Baba Muktananda, and Nityananda. May my gratitude always be measured by my attention and focus on your teachings. As well, friends of Siddha Yoga, in plain sight and hidden within these pages are many references to our beloved path. Look for them.

To my mother, who introduced me to Baba. I can only honor the immensity of your gift through the dedication of my life to all that continues to unfold from that mysterious, auspicious event.

To Mooch—thank you for *nothing and everything*. Words cannot go where you take me, but it's fun to try anyway and I know how much you love to play. I've done my best and will continue to do so. You have my word, and what are we without our word? How many forms you have! I am Yours and You are mine for eternity.

About Barron Steffen and Dr. Seana Lowe Steffen:

Barron Steffen is a longtime student on the spiritual path of Siddha Yoga, a big band crooner, and a widower. He has been a big wave surfer, a 1980s Italian pop singer, and an award-winning elementary school teacher. Steffen has now fully transitioned from the elementary school classroom to his company, *The Yoga of Mindset*, where he teaches children and adults how to use their thoughts so they're not used by them.

Dr. Seana Lowe Steffen founded the Restorative Leadership Institute (RLI). Her life's work in service to the possibility of a just and sustainable world continues there. Seana was the founding director of INVST Community Studies at the University of Colorado at Boulder where she designed and delivered interdisciplinary programs to develop engaged citizens and leaders working for the benefit of humanity and the environment. She co-founded the Rocky Mountain Youth Corps, was a certified UNITAR (United Nations Institute of Training and Research) climate change trainer, a Climate Reality Leadership Corps member, and participated as a credentialed guest at the International Women's

Earth and Climate Summit. In her human rights work, Seana was invited to facilitate the opening day for President Carter's Human Rights Defenders. Her podcast, *On Leading*, has featured climate scientist Dr. Katharine Hayhoe, oceanographer Dr. Sylvia Earle, and Green For All founder Van Jones. RLI received multiple "Best for the World" awards among all B Corps (certified B(enefit) Corp) across 50 countries, and they also created the *Seana Lowe Steffen Restorative Leadership Award* to be given yearly to a member of the global B Corp family who most embodies the spirit of restorative leadership—recognizing that everything is interconnected and that we act for the benefit of all. Seana was invited to be a Skoll World Forum delegate in 2016 and 2017, and co-authored several books:

- *Evolving Leadership for Collective Wellbeing: Lessons for Implementing the United Nations Sustainable Development Goals*
- *Innovation in Environmental Leadership: Critical Perspectives*
- *Engaging Classrooms and Communities through Art: The Guide to Designing and Implementing Community-Based Art Education*

For more information:
barronsteffen.com
theyogaofmindset.com
restorative-leadership.com